MEDITATION THROUGH PARABLES

GW00400121

Swami Anu

Swami Maunananda

Be Happy

मौज में रहो

Be Happy Inc. USA
Yo Veda Inc. Australia
Sat Bhavana Trust, India
Happy Folks of South Africa

INDRA PUBLISHING HOUSE

Indra Publishing House
...om

NEWHAM LIBRARIES
90800000065967

NEWHAM
PUBLIC LIBRARY
DYNIX:
INV. No.: 10756
LOC: S
CLASS: 158.12
90800000065967

Published by:

INDRA PUBLISHING HOUSE

Indra Publishing House
E-5/21, Arera Colony,
Habibganj Police Station Road,
Bhopal-462016
Phone : +91 755-4030921, 6462025
Telefax : +91 755-4059620
Email : manish@indrapublishing.com
pramod@indrapublishing.com
Web. : www.indrapublishing.com

© Sat Bhavana Trust, India
Be Happy Inc.USA
Yo Veda Inc. Australia
Happy Folks of South Africa
www.justbehappy.org

Price : 195/-
First Indian Print 2010
ISBN : 978-81-89107-73-4

Printed By:
Box Corugators And Offset Printers, Bhopal
& published by Mr. Manish Gupta for Indra Publishing House,
E-5/21, Arera Colony, Habibganj Police Station Road,
Bhopal 462016 INDIA

All rights reserved. No part of this book shall be reproduced or transmitted in any form or by any means, electronic, mechanical, magnetic, photographic including photocopying, recording or by any information storage and retrieval system, without prior written permission of the publisher. No patent liability is assumed with respect to the use of the information contained herein. Although every precau tion has been taken in the preparation of this book, the publisher and author assume no responsibility for errors or omissions. Neither is any liability assumed for damages resulting from the use of the information contained herein.

THE LAST WORD

In the beginning was 'Silence'. When it broke, sound manifested. Meaning given to the sound created the world of names and forms. Thus begins the *saṁsāra*. In this world of relative existence, a lot of efforts are put to go beyond by creating more and more words, sentences, books, CDs, cassettes and there is no limit to it. Although the intention is good, it leads to entanglement in the relative world and not freedom from the publications, talks, reading, discussing about the world and the Absolute. This creates the world of absolute chaos and subsequently getting lost in the world through words.

The Lord, out of His compassion relieved us of this entanglement through the deluge masterminded on 26th July, 2006 which took away the cause of absolute chaos through the relative world. Hence it was accepted as His will and no more publications of books in particular, will be produced in large quantities. The new printouts will be on laser print with few copies as per the requirement. Those interested may get them or visit our website (www.justbehappy.org) to read them.

This huge work of restructuring the publications is attributed to a collective contribution of a team of devoted seekers of Truth to whom we remain ever indebted.

SWAMI ANUBHAVANANDA

PREFACE

We go in search of peace and for that alone, we go with a hope to be happy. We try our best to change places to gain happiness. We try our best to wait for a change in time so that we can be happy and we also try our best to change the things and beings around us so that we should be happy. Alas! we forget to note that wherever we go, whenever we go and in whichever situation we go, "There we are!"

This "I" factor is the source of all that we have been searching for. Unfortunately, it was never focussed as an important parameter to work upon. The perception of the world by this 'I' depends on the quality of the mind which this 'I' has cultivated and nurtured; and ultimately developed, through a process of removal of *"māyopiyā"* of our 'I' (not the myopia of 'eye').

The surgery of this 'I' is being presented in this book of "Meditation Through Parables". After this surgery is complete, it is certain that we will rediscover our original vision and be able to see the inherent Divinity in and through our every experience. When we are able to discover Him and His expression in every experience, we are free from the disease of *"māyopiyā"* i.e. discover that this whole world is nothing but a play of *māyā* of the Lord and we are mere pawns in His game.

We are pleased to publish this wonderful work and hope that it will spread happiness everywhere.

In the Lord's service,

SAT BHAVANA TRUST

Sadguru Deva,
You are the inspiration
You are the thought,
You are the words,
I am but a poor instrument
Like *Kṛṣṇā's* flute.
Let my faith unto Your Feet
be ever wide awake.

INTRODUCTION

Meditation is not a part-time duty or a ritual to be practised everyday for a certain length of time. We have to be vigilant and develop a vision where in we are able to be in a meditative poise from every small or big experience that we go through in our daily life. This can be achieved if we are able to convert every experience into wisdom by learning from that experience. Normally, an average person gathers impression from each experience and thereby increases the load of these impressions on his mind in the form of good or bad memories.

In 'Medititation Through Parables,' an attempt is made to develop a faculty of light by working in the world lightly, so that each experience becomes the light of wisdom, and no more a load of going through good or bad experiences.

Each parable is selected from various spiritual literatures and recasted to convert the experience into wisdom. Wherever possible, sources are mentioned.

If we are able to read at random any parable at the beginning of the day and ruminate over it throughout the day, it will become an ideal start with a very healthy breakfast, to take up the loads of the day.

As with my other books, Saraswati Amma (now Swami Maunananda) has been the instrument who compelled me to work on it. The beautiful drawings for the parables were very intelligently and beautifully drawn by Brni. Nivedita Chaitanya of Australia who was a student of the Xth Vedanta Course at Sandeepany, Mumbai. My loving appreciation for both of them. May Lord Krishna bless them with a long and healthy life, and continue to express through them as ever.

The editorial skill of Shri. Vishwamitra Puri is fully reflected as in all my earlier publications. He is a God-sent gift to me, who is a rare combination of dedication and skill.

Sumati (Lakshmi) has done a great job of composing this book tirelessly, not only as a mechanical undertaking but as an intelligent seeker who has taken care of all the small details like spellings, transliteration, sanskrit composition etc.. Her devotion to the work and ultimately to spiritual pursuit is unparallel. I will be underestimating her devotion by expressing thanks for her invaluable contribution.

SWAMI ANUBHAVANANDA.

LIST OF THE SOURCES REFERRED

A. A.	*Amṛtānubhava*
A. B.	*Ātma Bodha*
A. G.	*Avadhūta Gītā*
Ast.G.	*Aṣṭāvakra Gītā*
B. A.	*Brahmānucintanam*
B. G.	*Bhagavad Gītā*
B. U.	*Bṛhadāraṇyaka Upaniṣad*
C. U.	*Chāndogya Upaniṣad*
D. D. V.	*Dṛg-Dṛśya Viveka*
D. M. S.	*Dakṣiṇāmūrti Stotram*
I. U.	*Īśāvāsya Upaniṣad*
K. U.	*Kaṭhopaniṣad*
Kai. U.	*Kaivalya Upaniṣad*
L. S. R.	*Life of Śrī Ramaṇa*
L. F. R.	*Latest From Ramaṇa Āśrama*
M. U.	*Muṇḍakopaniṣad*
N. B. S.	*Nārada Bhakti Sūtra*-s
N. D. M.	*Nisarga Datta Mahārāja's commentary*
P. D.	*Pañcadaśī*
S. U.	*Śvetāśvatara Upaniṣad*
S. S. S. C.	*Śrī Sāī Sat Caritā*
T. U.	*Taittarīya Upaniṣad*
T.W.R.M.	*Talks With Ramaṇa Maharṣi*
U. S.	*Upadeśa Sāram*
V. B.	*Vijñāna Bhairava*
V. C.	*Viveka Cūḍāmaṇi*
V. D.	*Vedānta Diṇḍimaḥ*
V. S.	*Vedānta Sāra*

Dedicated To All The Seekers Of Truth

1. THE DISCIPLE WHOSE FAITH IN HIS GURU WAS SHAKEN

***Guru* is He who dwells in one's heart, not in an external form only.**

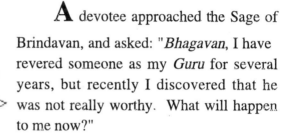

A devotee approached the Sage of Brindavan, and asked: "*Bhagavan*, I have revered someone as my *Guru* for several years, but recently I discovered that he was not really worthy. What will happen to me now?"

That sage replied: "One of two things will happen. If your faith is absolute, nothing will happen, nothing will change; if, on the other hand, you have taken him as an individual, who was born in a period of time, then your faith will be shaken, and you will be nowhere."

What helps us is not the external form of the *Guru*, but it is the *śraddhā* and the reverence associated with the *Gurutattva*. The *śraddhā* is not what he wants, but what we need. It is located in our mind, not in the object of reverence. With that faith, the *Guru* ceases to be a mortal with human frailties. He is then seen to reside in "my" heart. HE CAN NEVER BE IMPURE BECAUSE, MY HEART IS PURE. Discovery of Guru in one's own heart is meditation.

2. THE SAINT AND THE ORTHODOX PERSON

The universal expression of *Gurutattva.*

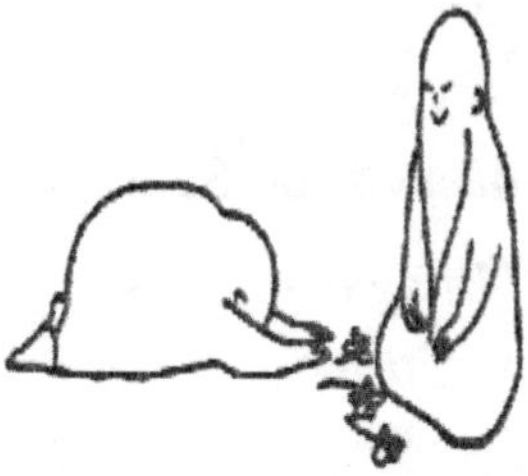

Once an orthodox *Agnihotri Brāhmin* was staying in *Śirdi.* One day *Bābā* sent a messenger to get some *dakśiṇā* (contribution) from him. The *Brāhmin* wondered why he, an orthodox *Brāhmin* who was the disciple of another Guru, should pay *dakśiṇā.*

However, he went to where *Bābā* was and standing at a distance threw flowers at *Bābā.* Then lo! and behold! he saw no *Bābā,* but his own Guru. Speechless, he fell at *Bābā*'s feet as he would at his Guru's. When he got up, he saw *Bābā*'s own blissful form, asking for *dakśiṇā.*

To consider only one particular form as the *Guru* is to strengthen the individuality and the body-identification. It only promotes *bheda bhāva,* that one's *Guru* is superior to the others. The same consciousness as *Gurutattva* expresses at different points. True and firm faith in one's *Guru* will ultimately lead one to see the universal expression of *Gurutattva* equally in all saints and sages.

[Adopted from S.S.S.C. XII]

3. THE DUMB PERSON AND HIS VOW

Being inseparably one with the *Guru,* the Truth.

A dumb person takes a vow of silence. But it does not mean anything; whether he takes a vow or not, he continues to be silent.

In the same way, it does not matter if the *jīvan mukta puruṣa* (One who is Realized) is in front of the Lord or away from Him, he is effortlessly one with Him.

Guru Tattva is not bound by individuality. *Guru* is all the time with his devotee, every moment, in every place.

When one is firmly established in this understanding, thereafter there is no more going away from, or coming nearer to the Divine, the *Guru*, the Truth. Perfect reflection and expression in the life of the disciple is meditation.

[Source: AA. IX. 43]

4. THE SAINT AND THE POTS

Receptivity to the *Guru*'s teaching is *Guru Seva.*

Once a visitor to an *Avadhūta* noticed that He was washing pots and placing them on the ground, mouth downwards. When asked why, the saint said, "Every pot coming to me comes with mouth downwards!" meaning thereby, that most people go to saints with an unreceptive attitude.

That disciple who is receptive to the *Guru Mahārājā*'s *upadeśa* (guidance), who imbibes the knowledge imparted by the *Guru*, renders true *sevā* (service) to Him. By reflecting on the *Guru*'s words deeply and by single-pointed meditation, he will be able to realize the Great *Guru Tattva* as the Truth, ever shining in his heart cave.

[Source: *Guru Gītā*]

5. THE MAN WHO TOOK HOLY DIP IN THE SEA

Taking refuge at the feet of the *Sadguru*

A man makes a *yātrā* (visit) to *Rāmeśvaram*, and plunges into the *sāgara* (sea) for a holy bath. Thereby he gets the merit of bathing in all the *tīrtha*-s (holy waters) and sacred rivers.

Similarly, when a man takes refuge at the feet of the *Sadguru*, he gets the merit of bowing to the Holy Trinity and also to *Parabrahman*. All distinctions and hostilities cease, great and small vanish. It is only the *Sadguru* who can take one across the ocean of *saṁsāra*, and makes one see the Lord in all creatures. Plunging deep below the three *guṇā-s* to discover the *sadvastu* - *sadguru* - The Reality, is meditation.

[Adapted from S.S.S.C. XXVII]

6. THE ELEPHANT AND THE DREAM-LION

Gurukaṭākṣa (mere look of the *Guru*) startles one to "wakefulness" to the truth

A wild elephant saw a lion in his dream. He woke up startled, and would not sleep again, lest the lion might appear again.

Similarly, in a man's life which is like a dream, the ego being the stubborn wild elephant, *śravana, manana* and *nidhidhyāsana* are the dream lion. They make the ego "wake up", but only for brief spells; he "goes to sleep" again. One day, he gets an intense, powerful and vivid dream called *GuruKaṭākṣa* (Lurer's kind look) which ejects him out of his slumber into full wakefulness and he gets *jñāna* (knowledge). Thereafter, there are no more dreams (of life); because he is wakeful at all times, alert, until true knowledge is obtained. Then he discovers that *GuruKaṭākṣa* was also only a dream-lion, that he alone was existing in all three states. In this ever existent state, even the feeling that *Guru* is different from him disappears.

[Source: LSR. 117]

7. THE GURU AND THE DISCIPLE

The *Guru Dakṣiṇa* of faith and peace.

There was once a *Guru* who was a great saint. He had a most devoted disciple who served him very long, never leaving him. The *Guru* was most merciful. He asked the disciple for only two rupee coins as *dakṣiṇā* (donation) which were given at once.

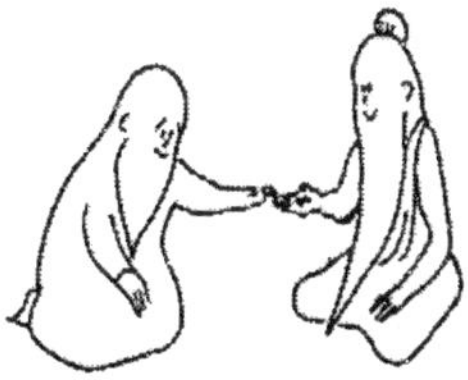

To the sincere seeker, the *Guru* is the sole refuge. Fixing the mind on Him, night and day, with no other subject to meditate upon, and with full faith, is one rupee of *dakṣiṇā* - *niṣṭhā* (dedication); the other rupee is *saburi* (patience). Patience removes all sins and afflictions, casts aside all fear, and leads to ultimate success. *Niṣṭhā* helps to demolish the wall of difference that separates the *Guru* from the disciple, until ultimately the distinction between *dhyātā, dhyeya* and *dhyāna* (meditator, the altar of meditation and meditation) get obliterated, and one merges with the *Guru* who is *Brahman*, the Pure Consciousness. When the disciple disappears in the presence of *Guru*, the meditation culminates in Self-Realisation.

[Adapted from S.S.S.C.]

8. THE STUDENTS WHO SOUGHT THE BRAHMAN

Importance of implicit faith in the *Sadguru.*

Four students of the scriptures were walking in a forest, discussing the nature of Brahman and how to realize it. The first advocated self-effort, the second - control of the mind, the third - discrimination between the real and unreal. The fourth one said: "Let us do our duty and surrender our body, mind and life itself to the *Guru* who is God." As the young men went rambling through the woods in search of God, a trader came by and enquired what they were looking for. They gave an evasive reply and were moving on when he offered them food and advised them to eat, rest and proceed. The first three declined; the fourth accepted the offer, moved by his kindness. Immediately, in place of the trader, the *Guru* stood before him and offered to show what he was seeking. The *Sadguru* took the young man to a well and hung him upside down with his hands dangling just above the water, and went away. He came back after several hours, took the young man out, and asked how he had fared. The young man replied that he was in supreme indescribable bliss. The *Sadguru* was so pleased that he took the young man under his care. The young man totally surrendered himself to the *Sadguru*, forgetting everything else.

When the senses and the mind are withdrawn from their objects (the water in the well), and are given a topsy-turvy direction, i.e. when they are introverted and fixed on the Self, the experience is of unalloyed, ineffable bliss. The *Sadguru*'s grace makes everything clear without one seeking and striving; self-realization flashes of itself. However learned one may be, one cannot traverse the Spiritual path without the *Guru*'s guidance, showing the right way and warning him of the pit-falls. *Guru* cannot but help the disciple. Hence full surrender to *Guru* is meditation.

[Adapted from S.S.S.C. XXXII]

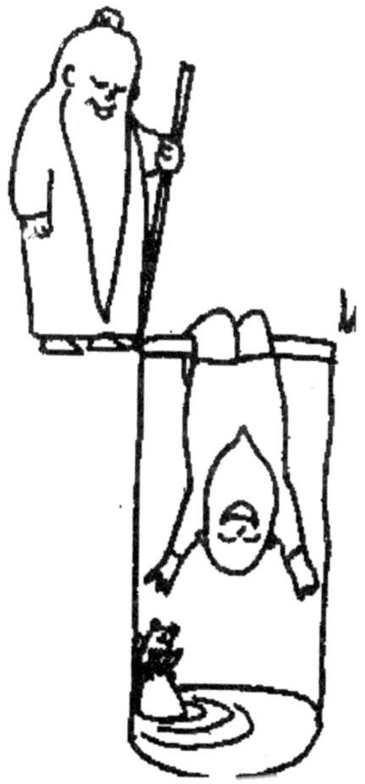

9. THE HELMSMAN OF THE FERRY BOAT

Absolute trust in *Sadguru* leads to eternal peace.

The helmsman of the boat ferries hundreds of people across the *Gangā* (Ganges River), morning and evening, to and fro from their places of work. They trust him absolutely to take them safely across.

In the same way, the true disciple trusts the *Sadguru* in getting him across the ocean of pains and sorrows of worldly existence. The *Sadguru* in his infinite compassion, endows his disciple with eternal knowledge and bliss. Faith strengthened with every experience is growth in meditation. When faith is no more required by the seeker, the knowledge is firm. This firm abidance in Self is meditation.

[Adapted from S.S.S.C. X]

10. THE MOTHER TORTOISE AND HER YOUNG ONES

Single pointed meditation on the *Guru* leads one to *Paramārtha* (Supreme Goal).

The mother tortoise is on one bank of the river, her young ones are on the other. She gives neither milk nor warmth, but her mere glance gives them nutrition. The young ones do nothing but remember their mother. Her glance is to them a downpour of nectar, the only source of sustenance and happiness.

In the same way, the *Guru*'s loving compassionate glance gives us happiness. There is no need for any *mantra* or *upadeśa*. Making the *Guru* the sole object of one's thoughts and actions, one attains the spiritual goal of life. Blessed is he who has firm faith and confidence in the *Guru*, believing fully that he is the Sole Actor or Doer. Blessed is he who knows the greatness of the *Guru*, and thinks him to be *Hari, Hara,* and *Brahma* incarnate. Seekers' efforts gets fulfilled by the last touch and push by the grace of the *Guru*. This helps in giving up efforts is meditation. Effortlessness is meditation.

[Source: S.S.S.C.]

11. THE TREES ON THE RIVERBANK

Transcience of Life

A mountain river is roaring down the gorges. As it rushes along, it eats up the sandy bankson either side, gradually uprooting the trees. Some trees had fallen earlier and have already been carried away; others are just falling in, and still others are leaning over perilously, and will be carried away soon.

In the same way, those from whom we were born, they are long dead; those with whom we were brought up, have also become objects of memory. Now, we ourselves are approaching our fallout day by day, hour by hour. Let us not further postpone our spiritual practice. Let us not waste a single moment of our life. Let us chant His name, His glory, do His work and contemplate on Him ! Let us start away before it is too late ! Our meditation has begun.

[Source: V.S. 48]

12. THE STONE THAT IS THROWN

Transcience of *karma phala* (Fruit of Action)

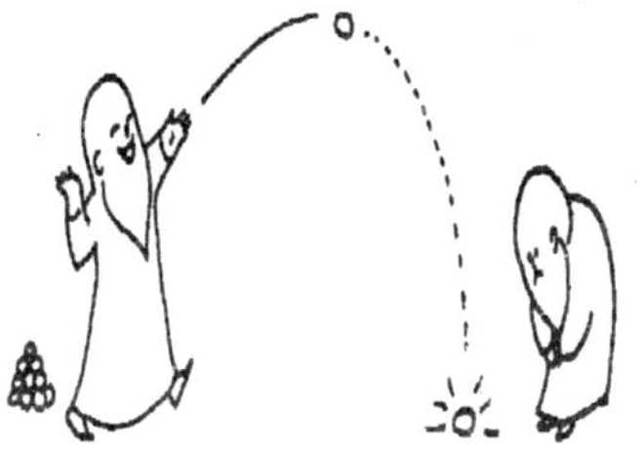

A stone is thrown. It will go only so far and so long as the energy associated with the throw lasts. This energy is determined in the parameter of time.

So also, the result of every action (*karma phala*) is conditioned by time. It is impermanent (*a-śāśvatam*). It only compels one to repeat the action in order to have repeated *karma phala*.

This is the *mahā udadi* (the great ocean) of *saṁsāra*, whose boundaries we do not know, nor its depth. One is lost without a sense of direction.

[Source: V.S. 2]

13. THE BOW AND ARROW

Action is inert.

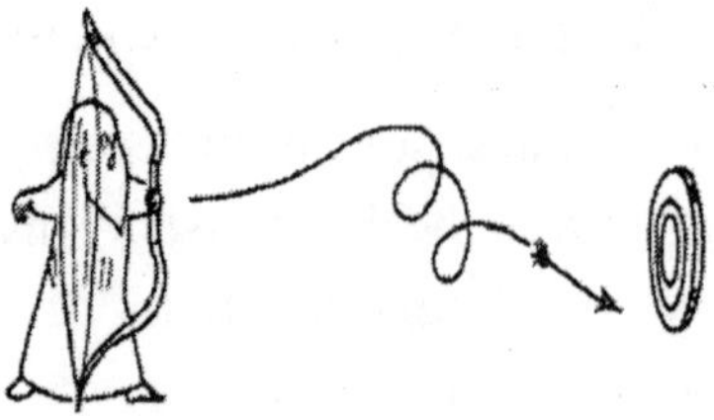

The arrow is propelled out of the bow but the movement of the arrow by itself is inert; it has no wisdom of choice.

The voice is amplified by the amplifier; but the voice itself is inert (*jaḍam*). In the same way, action by itself has no wisdom. It is inert.

Not to get lost in action is to enter the field of consciousness. Rise above the action and come to the actor! Then rise above the actor by remembering to do all acts for Him - The Consciousness. Journey from action to actor to Him for whom it is done, is meditation !

[Source: V.S. 1]

14.THE DREAM-LION

Waking up to the reality, the Self

A wealthy man retired to his comfortable bed one night after a good meal. Then he had a dream in which he was a destitute wandering in a jungle searching for food and shelter. Suddenly, he was pursued by a lion, and he ran and in order to save himself, he jumped into a river. The touch of the cold water woke him up only to find to his relief that he was safe in his own bed. As a dreamer, he had identified himself with his own mental creation of a destitute and suffered all those agonies. The moment he woke up, he rediscovered his own real identity.

In the same way, in our ignorance of our real nature, we start identifying ourselves with our ego-centric concepts that I am the body, I am the mind, the intellect etc.. Therefore, the conditions of the body, mind etc. become "my" conditions. To end this ignorance, one must "wake up" to the wisdom of our true identity-the self-the only Reality.

[Source: V.C. 27]

NEWHAM LIBRARY SERVICE

15. THE PARROT IN THE CAGE

The taste of freedom

A parrot is sitting in his cage, enjoying the fruit that he has been given. He eats and in between he talks cheerfully. He is imprisoned in the cage, but believes that his life is a happy one. One day, a boy comes and opens the cage door. The parrot hops out cautiously, takes one step, two steps, three ... lo! He flies out and up into the sky and now he understands what true freedom is.

In the same way, the *jīva* (individual self) is enslaved in this body and the *saṁsāra* (world), but is so hypnotized by the sense enjoyments that he cannot imagine any other life is possible. Only when the *Sadguru*'s Grace opens his eyes to a greater and larger life, that he understands how worthless his former limited existence had been. Discovery of higher and nobler possibility of life is the beginning of meditation.

[Source: S.S.S.C. XXIII]

16. THE KING UNDER A CURSE

Do not die a helpless death.

King *Parikṣit* was under a curse: he would die at the end of seven days bitten by a cobra. So he waited for the seventh day for death to claim him. *Parikṣit* spent every moment of his last seven days in listening to the glory of the Lord and thus lived in death by merging in Him, "far before the cobra of time" bit him.

For all of us, death is not far away. *"Na atidūre nṛṇām mṛtyuḥ."* Everyday is the seventh day. Therefore, engage yourself, only in the continuous contemplation on your own essential nature. *Brahma ekam pravicintyatām.* This is meditation.

17. THE HUNGRY MAN

Urgency to know the truth transcends all the considerations of do's and don'ts.

A man is very hungry. Satiation of that hunger is the sole concern on his mind. When he finds the food, he eats it immediately without ceremony, without worrying about propriety, etiquette etc. And the satisfaction of the hunger is instantaneous.

In the same way, when there is clarity about the goal and urgency to discover the Truth, all rules and regulations are swept aside. Things other than self-knowledge are of no consequence. Whatever you do or do not do, all the time in every experience, remind yourself constantly of your real nature. The rest is of no importance whatsoever. Urgency to know the Truth leads to intensity in meditation. Intensity in *sādhanā* (pursuit of the Self) dissolves all other problems and difficulties. To keep "knowing Truth" as the only priority in life is meditation !

[Source: P.D. VII. 114-5]

18. THE HOUSE ON FIRE

Waste not a moment in seeking the Supreme.

A house was on fire. The owner not having dug a well at the time the house was built, begins digging one now, so he can get water for putting out the fire! Of what avail is it?

Similarly, a wise person should put forth all his best exertions for the sake of the Supreme Truth, even while the body is free from disease, as long as senility is far off, the senses are unaffected and all the faculties are sharp. Not to wait till the best moment of emergency in life and to be ever- ready and alert in life about one's spiritual *sādhanā* (pursuit) is meditation !

19. THE MIRROR

Focused study of the scriptures.

Wanting to see his own face, a man asks for a mirror. His wife, the children and the servant, all rush to him, each with a mirror. But how many mirrors does he need to see his face?

Just one.

So also, one need not study too many books to know the Truth. Even one *upaniṣad* (scripture) studied in depth, reflected upon and practiced leads to the goal. An ounce of practice is better than tonnes of information gathered from the scriptures and the teacher which finally leads one into experience, is meditation.

[Source: P.D. IV. 47]

20. THE FARMER AT HARVEST TIME

Self-abiding is the goal and not mere erudition.

It is harvest time; the crop has been cut, The farmer separates the grain from the husk, and takes home only the grain. In the same way, a wise man, once he has gained direct and indirect knowledge of the self through study, reflection and contemplation, and attained firm abidance in the self, renounces all book knowledge and remains with his own essential nature. Books and study have no more relevance in that realm. Even knowledge of scriptures is only a memory. All memories are bondage. They only crystallize the ego.

The state of freedom is that where we forget all phenomenal experiences (sarvam vismaraṇam), and abide in the self (svāsthya). Forgetfulness of the world followed by focussing attention to the self is meditation.

[Sources: P.D. iv. 46 Ast. G. XVI-1]

21. THE MAN BITTEN BY A COBRA

Liberation is possible only by knowledge and not study only.

Once a man was bitten by a deadly cobra. In that moment of dire urgency, his only demand was for an antidote to kill the poison and restore him to health, no matter how, where from, with what attitude, the help was offered.

Similarly, the moment a seeker realizes that he has been bitten by the cobra of ignorance, he will have a sense of urgency to seek that knowledge of the Reality, to destroy that ignorance by the most direct means. He will not waste time in endless study and argument. Recognition of the limited experiences of this world to be the cause of sufferings, one opts for something unlimited. This option for seeking unlimited self is meditation.

[Source: V.C. 61]

22. THE LAMP AND DIAMOND

Even erroneous knowledge can lead to Liberation.

Two men walking in the darkness of night notice two bright light spots at a distance. Both run towards the sources of the two lights, thinking that both are diamonds. One finds only a lamp in the sanctum of a temple, the other finds a diamond.

The erroneous knowledge in both men was of the same quality. Neither was certain it was a diamond: in one case the *bhrama* (delusion) led only to a factual error and was only a lamp; in the other case, the *bhrama* led to a fruitful conclusion, he found the diamond. This is called *samvādi bhrama* (pursuit).

In the same way, even if a seeker has not strictly followed the *sādhanā* in prescribed sequence, his vedantik study does not go waste. His *upāsanā* of *Brahma Tattva*, even if it is an error of judgment, does lead to the right conclusion, viz. the understanding of his own essential nature by the method of *samvādi bhrama.*

Similarly, the words *sat-cit-ānanda* do not really indicate the Truth; but contemplation on their meaning I am *sat* which is not as opposed to *anatmā,* leads one to the point where knowledge is revealed. This is intentional *samvādi bhrama.* Chanting the mantra of the Lord's name, even if practised without understanding does lead to the realisation of Truth. Hence, chanting the Lord's name with every respiration is meditation, even if done without any understanding

[Source: P.D. ix.1-13]

23. THE ANT THAT FELL INTO THE RIVER

Lord's grace descends on the *jīva* (individual being) without logic or reason.

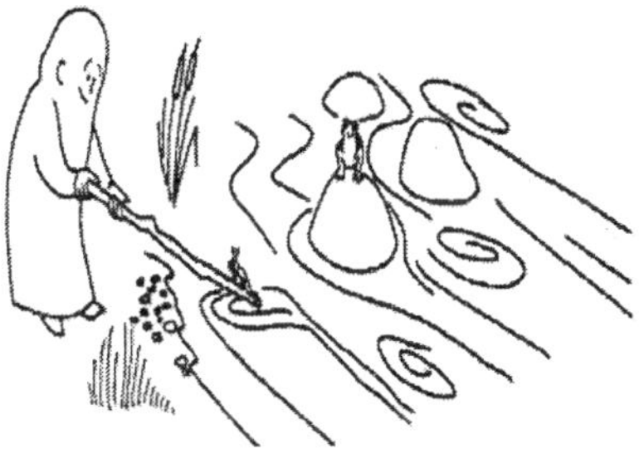

A tree stood on a river bank, its branches bending low over the running water. An ant on one of the branches slipped and fell into the river below. The poor struggling ant was swept from one whirlpool to another. Then, suddenly, a compassionate person passing by, happened to notice the struggling ant. He took pity on it, and by means of a stick lifted the ant out of the water and dropped it high up on the bank, safe from the running water.

In the same way, the *jīva* migrates from one life to another in an endless cycle of birth and death, without redemption. Then by the Grace of the Lord, when some *puṇya karmā* (meritorius deeds) done somewhere, sometime in the past lives, is ready for fructification, a saint or sage comes into the life of the struggling seeker, for no logic or reason, and lifts him out of the current of *saṁsāra*. When we go beyond cause and effect, the Lord alone remains. When His Grace prevails, only then do things happen, not because of one's cleverness. Once this Knowledge is firmly rooted, then there is *viśrānti*, a relaxed, cheerful acceptance of whatever happens in life. Ability to drop the cause and effect enquiry in life is the beginning of meditational poise in the seeker.

[Source P.D. I. 30-31]

24. THE BIRD WHO HAS BUILT ITS NEST ON A HEIGHT

Discrimination and dispassion alone can lead to Self - Realisation.

A bird built its nest on a tree which was on top o f a steep rock. To reach its nest, it had only one method - to spread both its wings and soar high above the earth and all its dangers.

Similarly, the earnest seeker who aspires to soar high to the Supreme Pinnacle of the Truth, must develop strong wings of *viveka* (discrimination) and *vairāgya* (dispassion). Unless both are equally strong, he cannot be immune against objects, emotions and thought that tantalize and disturb the mind.

Only thus can he gain liberation from the bondages of *saṁsāra*, and experience the bliss which is independent of all external factors. He revels in his own Self. To dive deep in the depths of *cidākāśa* is meditation.

[Source: V.C.375-6]

25. THE MAN WHO WANTED INSTANT BRAHMAJÑĀNAM

He who seeks God must forsake money.

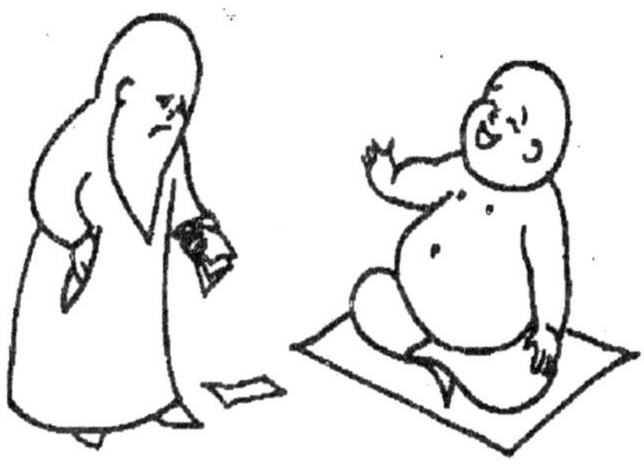

A rich, avaricious man once went to *Śirdi Bābā* and asked for quick *Brahma Jñāna* (Supreme Knowledge) because he thought that, with that acquisition, his life would be complete.

The saint understood the situation. Saying that it was indeed rare to find a person who sought that Supreme Knowledge, he assured the visitor that he would show *Brahman* to him. After some time, he sent a messenger to a grocer to get a loan of five rupees. The boy returned to report that the shop was closed. He sent the boy to a second person and then to a third, and each time received a negative reply. In the meanwhile, the visitor grew impatient and urged *Bābā* to show him *Brahman* without delay as it was getting late for him.

The saint smiled and replied, "My dear friend, I have been showing you all along and you haven't understood. In your pocket is a bundle of five-rupee notes and you watched me ask for a mere five rupee loan, but you could not part with one note. How can one whose mind is engrossed in wealth, progeny and prosperity expect to know *Brahman* without first removing his attachment to them?

For knowing *Brahman*, the Self, one has to surrender five things (symbolized by the five rupees): the five pranas, the five senses, the mind, the intellect and the ego. He who has not turned away from worldly objects, whose senses are not subdued, whose mind is not quietened, cannot find *Ātma Jñāna* (Self Knowledge). One who seeks the Truth can permit no compromise. Only to him who has put away all desires from his mind, whose spirit finds comfort only in itself, will the Truth be revealed. With the end of wordly thoughts is the beginning of meditation.

[Source: S.S.S.C. xvi-xvii]

26. THE MAGICIAN AND HIS BEAUTIFUL CREATIONS

***Doṣa dṛṣṭi* (critical appraisal) removes all enchantment for worldly objects.**

A magician at one of his shows, created beautiful things by his magic; they appeared so real. He invited the audience to come and pick up anything they liked. But the audience merely sat in their seats and smiled. No one desired anything from that creation, knowing it to be unreal.

Similarly, a wise man, once he has inquired into the nature of worldly objects and recognized that they are mere appearances in a state of ignorance, will he ever desire anything? His critical appraisal (*doṣa dṛṣṭi*) reveals their faults; he will not be enchanted by them any longer. There will be neither a desire nor a desirer. Annihilation of desire and the desirer is meditation.

[Source: P.D. VII. 137-8]

27. THE HUNGRY MAN WHO WAS OFFERED POISONOUS FOOD

Devalue the world

A person was suffering from severe pangs of hunger. The only food available was a fruit which was known to be poisonous. Knowing the nature (the *doṣa*) of that fruit, will he ever take it?

So also, one who has understood the fallacy of worldly enjoyments and who has discovered the joy of his own being, why will he ever go to worldly enjoyments, and why will he allow himself to be drowned in the sorrow resulting from such attachments? Devalued world alone can be impotent and does not influence the seeker. Such an undisturbed person is ever in meditation.

[Source: P.D. vii. 142]

28. THE GARBAGE COLLECTOR

Self-Inquiry is the collective rejection of not-self.

The garbage collector gathers the garbage from point to point and collectively throws them in the dump yard. He does not waste his time in examining what are its contents.

In the same way, it is fruitless for one who wants to know one's Self to count the number and nature of *tattva-s* (matter), which are veiling the Self and which are the nature of not-self. Instead, he should just collectively cast them all aside. One should only consider one's whole life in this world to be like a dream. We do not discard the dream part by part, but in its whole. So too the waking world be discarded in its totality and not in parts. This ability is meditation.

[Source: The Path of Sri Ramana I App.I]

29. THE BOY WHO DREAMS OF A TIGER

Paramātmā (Supreme Self) associated with the gross body becomes a deluded _jīva_ (individual being).

A boy lay awake in bed, imagining a tiger walking up and down in a zoo. He was not afraid because he knew that the tiger was only a projection of his mind. Then he dropped off to sleep and in his dream, the same tiger appeared, but now it seemed very real and threatening a nightmare.

The sensible waker had become a deluded individual in the dream, the dreamer.

In the same way, when the *Paramātmā*, who is *akartā* and *abhoktā* becomes identified with the physical body, he becomes a deluded *jīvātmā*. He was the supporter of the universe, now he is the supported, dependent on the universe. The infinite becomes limited; the eternally blissful becomes a *duḥkhī*. But the *Paramātmā* is ever the *Paramātmā*; the *jīvātmā* is only the nightmare experienced in the dream, that is the *jāgrat avasthā* (waking world).

[Source: Kai.U. 12]

30. THE BOY CIRCLING ROUND A PILLAR

Delusion of *māyā* (illusion) creates appearances of names and forms.

A boy goes circling round and round a pillar in play. He sees the world also as circling round and round; the sky appears to contain a hundred moons.

Similarly, the *jīva* being deluded by *māyā*, sees the world as full of various names and forms. Stop the movement of mind as thoughts and the world along with its sorrows disappears. Thoughtfree knowledge is freedom from knowledge. This is meditation.

[Source: D.M.S, M.U. VIII-24]

31. THE KING WITH UNSATIABLE DESIRE

Actions done for fulfilment of desire leads to *saṁsāra.*

Once there was a King who loved life so much that even though he grew old, his appetite for worldly enjoyments was unsatiated. He did penance and obtained a boon by which he could exchange his old age for youth with anyone who was willing to sacrifice his own youth for the sake of the old King. At last, taking pity on his father, the King's youngest son gave his youth to his father, and took over the father's old age. After enjoying extended youth for a long long time, at last one day, wisdom dawned on the King. He realized the ephemeral nature of enjoyments, and his own folly and selfishness.

In the same way, one who sees the fickle and transient nature of these enjoyments, understands the futility of action for the fulfilment of such desires. Let all actions be done only as worship to the Lord. Then it will not bind. It will not result in the entanglement of *saṁsāra* (illusory world).

[Source: V.D. 14]

32. THE STORY THE NANNY TOLD

The world is only a creation of the mind.

A nanny told the following story to a child:

"In a non-existent city, there lived three princes: of them, two were unborn and the third was not conceived. They started on a journey and reached three trees, of which two did not exist, and the third was not planted!

After eating the fruits of those trees, they went on and reached the banks of three rivers: two were dry, and in the third there was no water. The princes had a good bath and quenched their thirst. They then reached a big city which was about to be build. They found three palaces, of which two had not been built, and the third had no walls. They entered the palace and found three gold plates. Two were broken and the third was pulverized. They took 99 minus 100 grams of rice and cooked it. They invited three holy men to be their guests. Two had no bodies, the third had no mouth. After the holy men had eaten, the princes partook of what was left and lived happily ever after."

The child was so thrilled by the story that he went happily to sleep, thinking of the three princes.

The creation of the world is as real as this story. The world is no more than an idea in consciousness. It is only created out of the mind's imagination. Those who are immune to inquiry like that child, for them the world is valid. REJECT THE ERROR OF IDEATION AND BE FREE FROM IDEAS. Perception followed by projection is *saṁsāra* (illusory world). Perception without projection is freedom! To live in freedom is meditation.

[Source: Yoga V -utpattiprakaranam III 101]

33. THE COW THAT IS TETHERED TO A PEG

The world of names and forms have meaning only with reference to the centre 'I'.

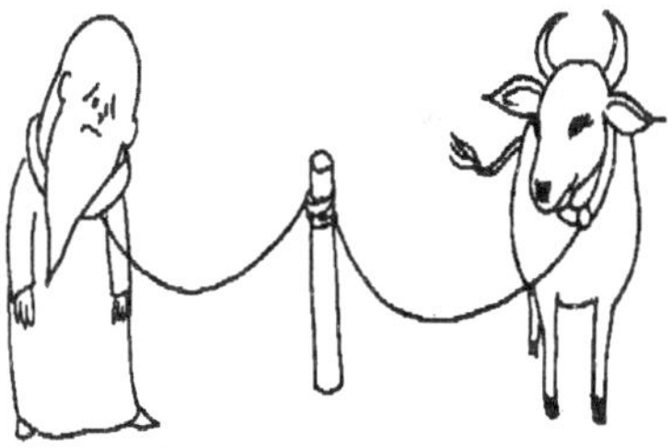

A cow is tethered to a peg by a long rope. It goes round and round in circles, grazing, as far out as the length of the rope will permit. The longer the rope (the radius), the wider the circumference ad infinitum until it becomes a circle without a circumference but with the center everywhere.

In the same way, each one of us is the same center, although it appears to be different from point to point; and the circumference which seems to limit the centers has no existence. The circumference cannot be born without a center, but the center is independent of the circumference. The limitation of the circumference has no reality. The total world of names and forms has meaning only with reference to this **'I'**, the center. If **'I'** the center is not there, the circumference of wife, children, possessions, beliefs etc. cannot be. Every **'My'** is dependent on **'I'**. But the self is not conditioned by any limitation of dharma or *sampradāya* (organised unit).

[Source: M.U. 1.1.6]

34. THE WOOD AND THE FIRE

World is an expression of seer and seen.

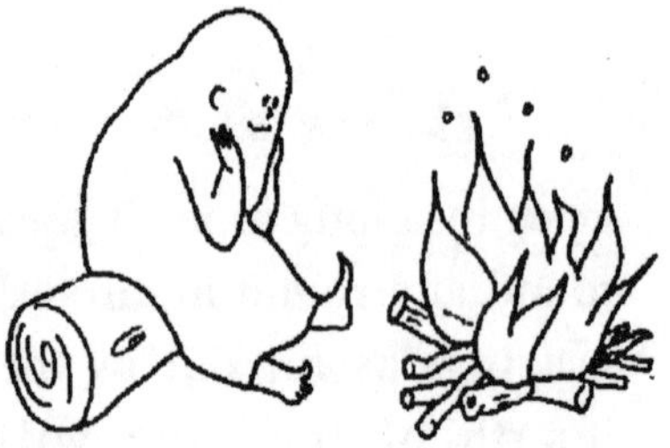

In wood, fire is un-manifest. When fire becomes manifest, it expresses as heat and light. When it is un-manifest, both are withdrawn.

In the same way, the Pure Consciousness 'I', remains un-manifest and undivided as seer and seen. Just as the fire can manifest either as heat or as light, the consciousness has the freedom to express either as seer (*dṛg*) or as the seen (*dṛṣya*).

When the divided consciousness is taken as real, there is entanglement in the world in the form of duality. When all the distinctions are withdrawn, one merges in the un-manifest one-ness.

[Source: V.D. 30]

35. THE SINGER AND HIS SINGING

Creation is no creation.

A singer is giving a performance. The accompaniments are tuned; the audience is expectant. What does he do? He closes his eyes, and 'lets go' his singing potentiality. A singer is not born; only his 'singing' is.

In the same way, the Absolute *Param Tattva*, out of its free will, its svatantrata or freedom, "lets go" of the universe. This "letting go" is not creation. It is as much creation; as the past, present and future waves are creations of the ocean. Disappearance of the meditator during meditation is true meditation.

[Source: B.A. 22-24]

36. THE MARUMARĪCIKĀ (MIRAGE)

Reality and myth are the same.

A man walking on a desert road at noon on a summer day, sees water shimmering at a distance. He runs towards it to cool himself, only to find that it is only an appearance of water (a mirage), not real water.

He walks on. The mirage does not disappear even after knowing it to be so. The appearance continues to be, only now the man does not run to it for water.

In the same way, the phenomenal world is a myth. Even after knowing it, it continues to appear. It appears only in the presence of the cognizing self. Therefore the self is the Reality. As the Self, the world is real; apart from the Self, it is a myth. To perceive the world as apart from the Self is wrong. Therefore, three statements should be taken together: Brahman is real; the world is a myth; Brahman is the world. Recognition of the Self to be transcendental and immanent simultaneously, is meditation.

[Sources: TWRM. 315 & V.C. 123]

37. THE MAN WHO DREAMT THAT HE WAS KING

The waking world is as unreal as the dream world.

A man had a dream in which he was a king, possessing and enjoying everything that he desired. He dreamt that he had a big army with whose help he conquered his enemy.

Later he was defeated by another king, retired to the forest and lived a life of austerity for a long, long time. But when he woke up, he realized that the dream had lasted only a very short span of time.

In the same way, in the waking state, man rules over the 'kingdom' which his mind imagines and does not see how his life is being destroyed by the river of time. The experiences of the waking state are as meaningless as those of the dream state. When spiritual awakening comes, the waking state experiences also disappear as null and void. Immunity to wordly inflictions is meditation.

[Source: D.M.S., M.U.: 1.16 to 18]

38. THE DREAMER WHO WAKES UP

Saṁsāra is not an objective reality

A dreamer dreams a dream. In the dream world, he experiences pleasures and pains. Then he wakes up. He loses all interest in the dream world because it was only a part of himself, and was not different from him.

So it is, with the waking world also. It ceases to interest us once we wake up from this waking dream (*saṁsāra*), and realize that it was indeed a part of ourselves, and not an objective reality.

When we think that the objects are apart from us, we desire them. If we understand that all objects are only a thought form, we would no longer desire them.

We are the water, and all objects are bubbles in it. The bubbles cannot exist apart from the water. Inclusion of everything in the definition of 'I' is meditation.

[Source: TWRM. 625]

39. THE SPIDER AND ITS WEB

Creation is the Supreme Reality itself.

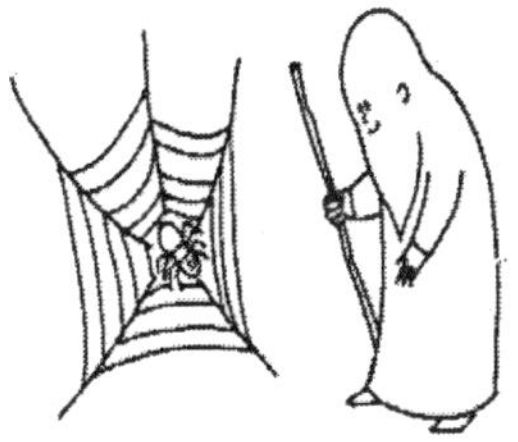

The spider starts to build a new web for itself. It creates the threads needed for the web out of itself. The material for the web is the very substance of the spider. Thus the spider is both the material and the efficient cause of the web simultaneously; unlike as in the mud pot where mud is the material cause and the pot-maker is the efficient cause.

In the same way, the whole world is created out of the *Akṣara Tattva*, the *Brahman* Itself. *Brahman* is only one and one without a second and *abhinna* (undifferentiated). And he is simultaneously both the material cause (*upādāna kāraṇa*) and efficient cause (*nimitta kāraṇa*). Thus the two causes are in reality one, not two: one aspect becomes the world, the other aspect becomes the maker of the world. So *Paramātmā* is called '*abhinna nimitta upādāna kāraṇam*'. So, in and through creation, *Brahman* alone is. There is nothing else other than Brahman. Thoughtfree experience of non-duality in every experience is meditation.

40. THE RIVER AND THE WAVES

The Self alone is the substratum of all names and forms.

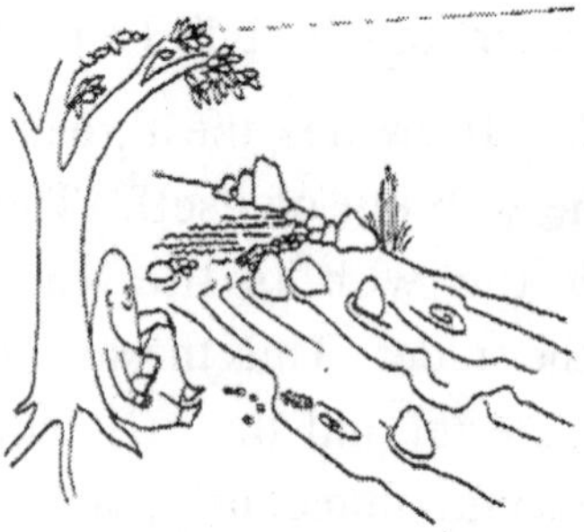

The big, vast, deep River Ganga is running miles and miles. On it, rise and play many waves, big and small. They rise, stay awhile and subside. But the river is totally uninfluenced and undisturbed by any wave. However, without the river, not a single wave can be.

In the same way, I, the Pure Consciousness alone is the substratum of the total world of Names and Forms. I, the substratum, is the Reality. The names and forms that appear in this world do not limit me. I am *adṛśyam* (non-seeable). All that is seen will change; all that which changes will be destroyed; but I am the one who is present in every change, yet remains changeless. Being the substratum, how can I like or dislike any name or form? Can I dislike any part of my body? I am in every part. Where there is oneness, *rāga* and *dveṣa* are not possible. It is *nirviśeṣa prema* (pure love). The ability to extend pure love towards the whole universe (as we love oneself the most), is a state of meditation.

[Source: M.U. 1.1.6]

41. THE KING AND THE JUGGLER

The world is the play of the mind.

A juggler entered the court of a King and with a wave of a bunch of feathers brought a cavalier on a beautiful horse. He said: "O King, ride on this horse around the world."

The King closed his eyes, and when he opened them, he began to tremble and was about to fall down. His ministers supported him and asked: "What delusion has over powered you? Only those who are attached to trivial objects and false relationships succumb to mental aberration."

The King said: "I had a strange hallucination in which I rode a horse through a desert, married a tribal woman, begot children, and sank to a sinful life. A famine struck the country and my family starved. Unable to see my youngest child suffer from hunger, I offered him my flesh. He said: 'Give me'. As I was about to enter the pyre, I woke to my senses."

The world of appearance is nothing but the play of the mind (the juggler). It is able to delude even men of wisdom by veiling the real nature of the self. Destroy this illusion by discrimination and wisdom, and rest in peace. Not yielding to the mischief of the mind and its suggestion is meditation.

[Source: Yoga Vāsiṣṭa II 103-109]

42. THE SHIP-WRECKED TRADER

When the mind is at rest, the world of plurality rolls away.

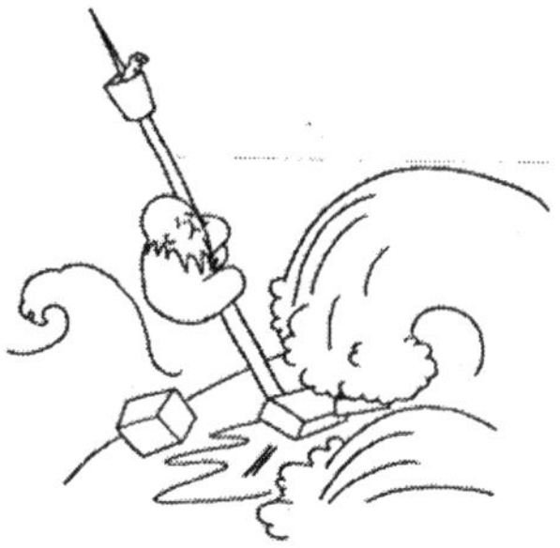

A trader was crossing the seas with all his merchandise, from port to port, transacting business, gathering new experiences and gaining wealth. One day, his ship was caught in a storm, and when the storm abated, it was seen that the ship along with the trader and merchandise had sunk.

Similarly, in the limitless ocean of the Self, the *jīva* (the trader) travels from *janma* to *janma* (birth to birth), in the ship of the world of names and forms, transacting business in worldly experiences, and gathering more and more *vāsanā-s* (the riches).

Till at last, when the storms of the mind have abated, the ego along with the collected merchandise of *vāsanā*-s get sunk. What is left is just the shore-less glory of the Infinite Self. When we learn from our experiences, good or bad, we do not gather impressions on our mind called *vāsanā-s.* A constant process of learning, not leaving any impressions on the mind, is meditation.

[Ast. G. II 24]

43. TWO FATHERS AND THEIR SONS

Pleasure and pain are only mental projections

Two young friends left their village and went to a distant place in search of employment. One took ill and died. The other sent a message through someone who was going past his village, to inform his own father about the death. Somehow, the messenger got the names mixed up with the result that the father of the living son believed him dead, and bemoaned his imagined loss; while the other father rejoiced that his son was alive and well (although he was really dead).

In this way, pleasure and pain have no relation to reality. They are only mental projections. They are the cause of bondage. *sarvasya jīvasya bandhkṛt mānasam jagat.* The ability to keep information reaching us through the mind's weakness or wrong perceptions, without any influence is meditation.

[Source: TWRM. 614 P.D. iv. 35]

44. RAHU SWALLOWING THE SUN

Mind veils the apprehension of Reality.

When the moon comes between the earth and the sun, the phenomenon called solar eclipse occurs. It is said that Rahu, a demon with a head and no body, has swallowed the sun! Because the sun is so far away, the moon is nearer, and man on the earth is so much smaller than both, it appears as though the moon is obstructing the vision of the sun. If one could rise above the moon, there would be no eclipse at all. And of course for the sun, nothing has swallowed him, nothing has covered him.

In the same way, it is the mind (the moon), that is coming between me and the Self (the Sun), and is veiling the glory of the Self from me. Mind is the manifestation of ignorance (avidyā), the non-apprehension of the Reality. Transcend the mind, and end all pluralistic perception. Have the direct vision of (realize) the Self. All sufferings because of the veiling (the eclipse) will end. Thought free experience of one's own independent curious, blissful existence is meditation.

[Source: V.C. 139.]

45. THE AGONIZING MAN IN A GREAT FOREST

The mind is its own source of sorrow.

In a great big forest lived just one person with many limbs. He was ever restless, beat himself with a mace, ran away from his own beating, then fell into a well, came out and again beat himself, then ran into a banana grove and wept and cried and ran and beat himself ...Then others also came and did likewise.

"I" advised them to abandon such ignorant ways. Some accepted and became enlightened; others ignored the advice and continued to suffer.

This world is the forest. It is the life of the worldly man with numerous thorns of family, wealth, etc. The person with many limbs is the mind with its many manifestations. The mind punishes itself by its own tendencies. The well is hell and the banana grove is heaven, between which the mind keeps flitting.

Ignorance makes one hurt oneself out of one's own volition, and we run hither and thither in panic. 'I' is the light of inquiry, which shines in everyone's heart, yet one wanders, driven by desire. An uncontrolled mind is the source of sorrow. When this is understood through inquiry, the sorrow vanishes.

[Adapted from: Yoga Vāsiṣṭha III 98-99]

46. CORN IN THE HAND-MILL

Introverting the mind is *sādhanā*.

Once Kabir, seeing a woman grinding corn wept. His Guru asked him: "Why do you weep?"

Kabir replied: "Guru Maharaja, I weep because I feel the agony of being crushed by the mill of earthly existence like the corn in the hand-mill."

The Guru replied:

"Do not be afraid; hold fast to the handle of knowledge of this mill; do not wander far away from it; but turn inward to the center, and you are sure to be saved."

Living at the periphery of our personality is sorrow. Coming to the centre of our Being is freedom. This journey from the periphery to the centre is Meditation.

[Source: S.S.S.C.]

47. THE BALL THAT BOUNCED DOWN THE STAIRS

The fall of the extroverted mind.

A boy is playing with a rubber ball on top of the stairs on the third floor. Accidentally, in a moment of carelessness, the ball slipped from his hand and fell down the stairs. It went bumping down, sometimes two steps at a time, at others several steps, but always down, down and down till it reached the ground.

In the same way, even a man of wisdom can fall if he neglects his steady attunement with the Self. If through inadvertence, he forgets his real nature, and allows his mind to become extroverted, it is the beginning of an irreversible fall. The mind reaches a state of utter ruin, far away from the Self. The seeker should therefore be ever vigilant to guard against this "Self-forgetfulness".

[Source: V.C. 322-9]

48. THE STRAYING COW

The mind turned inwards finds happiness.

A cow was accustomed to graze stealthily on others' pastures. She could not be confined to her stall. Her keeper tried hard to tempt her with luscious grass and fine fodder. She refused the first time, nibbled the next time, but soon her innate tendency to stray asserted itself and she slipped away. Gradually and patiently, by constant cajoling and tempting, she got accustomed to her stall. And finally, even if let loose, she would not stray away.

Similarly with the mind. It has so long been accustomed to wander and stray that it cannot be turned inward easily. Only by long and repeated practice and by dispassion, can it be brought under control. Once it finds its inner happiness, it will not thereafter wander outward.

[Source: TWRM. 213]

49. THE LAMP IN THE ROOM

Importance of the mind in *sāttvik vṛtti* (impurity free thought).

A lamp is placed in a room. It has both heat and light as its aspects, but its light alone pervades the room, not the heat. This does not mean there is no heat in the lamp.

In the same way, the *Ātmā*, the *Sākṣi* is of the nature of *Cidānanda*, i.e. it is both *cit svarūpa* (consciousness), and *ānanda svarūpa* (bliss). However, with reference to the thought, only the *cetanatā* or consciousness aspect manifests, not the *ānanda* aspect. The reflecting medium i.e. the mind or thought does not allow the manifestation of *ānanda.*

When the thoughts are *sāttvik*, i.e. when they are free from impurities, then there is identity between consciousness and bliss, and both are experienced simultaneously. *Sāttvik sukham* is where *cit* and *ānanda* manifest together, where loss and gain, knowledge and ignorance, action and inaction are irrelevant.

[Source: P.D. XII-74-78]

50. THE BIRD CAUGHT IN A NET

Technique for converting the liability of the mind into an asset .

A bird has been caught in a hunter's snare. Try as it might to escape, the net holds it down and quietens its fluttering. However, the moment the strings are cut, the bird flies away.

So also the mind is like the ensnared bird (*jālapakṣivat*). By itself, it is always restless and fluttering. It can be quietened (*laya*) when caught in the snare of breath-control (*prāṇāyāma*). But this *laya* or quietening is only temporary. It lasts only so long as the discipline (net) of *prāṇāyāma* is operative. The moment the breath-control is stopped, the mind will fly away from the *laya*, and start fluttering again. A more enduring way to make the mind abide in the Heart is to contemplate on the source of all thoughts and reach the substratum that Self is! By this contemplation, the negative habit of projection followed by every perception will be destroyed and the mind is no more a liability.

[Source: V.S. 11]

51. THE LAMP KEPT IN A SHELTERED PLACE

Achieving the movement-less mind.

A lamp is kept in a sheltered niche where the wind cannot disturb it. It does not flicker; it is absolutely still. Although it has the potentiality to flicker and change, yet it is still.

In the same way, *Paramātmā* (supreme self) has all the potentiality to reflect, to move, to change, to manifest at will. He is *cit svarūpa*. Yet he maintains the original unchanging position of *śivattva* (auspiciousness).

He who has arrived at the point of *aparokṣa anubhūti* of his own essential nature (*śiva eva asmi kevalah*), his mind is perfectly still, without the slightest movement.

[Source: D.D.V.]

52. THE IRON PIECE IN THE FIRE

The ego borrowed consciousness from Self.

An iron rod is placed in the fire. Slowly, it absorbs the heat and luminosity of the fire, and after a sufficiently long time, it is difficult to tell the iron and the burning coal apart. At the beginning, the iron was heavy, cold and black, and the burning fire was light, golden and hot. But now, the qualities of the fire and iron have been mutually transferred.

Similarly, when the not-self (the matter) is in contact with the Self (the Consciousness), it acquires the semblance of consciousness through mutual superimposition. From the "Infinite", the finite "appears" to emerge. From the substratum, the knower and known manifest. They are only a play of the consciousness. Once they are withdrawn from the Self, they are seen to be what they are -- false and unreal. The Self alone is, and it never changes.

[Sources: V.C. 350-1, D.D.V. 226]

53. THE "DEAD" CITRON TREE

Ego's tendency to rise up again and again.

A garden-lover had planted a citron tree in his garden and was tending it carefully and regularly. Once he had to go away for some days. On his return, he found to his dismay that the tree appeared as if it had totally dried up. Not giving up hope, he continued watering the tree regularly. After several days, he found to his great relief and delight that the tree which had looked dead, had revived and sprouted leaves and flowers again.

In the same way, by conquering the ego, one should not become complacent or lax. The mind must ever be kept under vigilant control so that it does not ruminate over sense objects and let those dominate his life again. Let every extroverted thought, as it arises, be sublimated to Divine thought.

"Tad arpita akhila ācāraḥ san kāma-krodha-abhimāna-ādikam tasmin eva karaṇīyaṁ."
"Dedicate all activities to Him; all of one's desires, anger, pride etc. should be turned towards Him alone."

[Sources: V.C. 310, N.B.S. 65]

54. SOAP-NUT POWDER ON WATER.

Death of individuality in Self-Knowledge.

It is the rainy season; waters are muddy. To remove the dirt, soapnut powder (*kaṭaka reṇu*) is sprinkled on the surface. The powder forms a thin film and as it slowly settles down at the bottom carrying all the mud particles with it, it leaves the water clear. Thus, not only the dirt goes down but the cleaning agent itself is also removed with it.

Similarly, the Self is present at all times, pure and without blemish. But it is contaminated by ignorance and consequent agitation. To remove these impurities, it is necessary to clean the mind with the soapnut powder of meditation. The mind becomes extremely subtle; the dirt of wrong identifications is removed along with the meditation itself, which is only *vṛtti jñānam* (knowledge of thoughts). Finally, the meditation also disappears and one's own essential nature, the Pure Self, alone remains.

[Sources: A.B. 5, TWRM. 624]

55. THE MAN WITH THE THORN IN HIS THROAT

Destruction of the ego gives the freedom to enjoy *ātma sukham* (self bliss)

A man was very hungry, and a rich fare (a wide variety of food) was placed in front of him. But he could not eat or appreciate the tasty food, because a thorn was stuck in his throat.

Similarly, so long as the thorn of the ego is in us, we cannot enjoy the Bliss of Infinitude which is plenty everywhere. It is only when all thoughts connected with the *ahaṁkāra* are cut asunder with the sword of Realization, that we can gain the liberty to enjoy the Bliss of the Self (*Ātma-sāmrājya sukham*).

[Source: V.C. 307]

56. THE THREE DEMONS

Absence of ego makes one immortal

Once there was a demon who was a terror to the Gods. In order to protect his forces, he created three new demons. Since they had no previous incarnation, the three demons were totally free from ego-sense and mental conditioning. Therefore, they had no fear, doubt, desire, anger etc.. This made them invincible. The Gods were helpless. So they lay low and bided their time.

As fighting continued against the Gods, gradually, the sense of "I am" was created in the demons; desires, fears and confusion followed. They lost their invincibility and were defeated.

Those in whom the ego-sense does not exist, know neither desire nor anger, and are immortal. The one Infinite Consciousness, which is of the nature of pure bliss, entertains the notion of "I am" and then gets eclipsed by the shadow of ego-sense and gets a distorted image of itself. Therefore, one should abandon this ego-sense and be established in the conviction that "I is nothing".

57. THE PHILOSOPHER KING AND THE SAGE

Annihilation of the ego is being in Self-dom.

Janaka, the philosopher king, one day heard a *puṇḍit* (priest) say that knowledge of *Brahman* can be gained in as short a time as is taken for 'placing the second foot on the second stirrup after having put the first foot in the first stirrup'.

The King wanted this statement demonstrated and proved, and finding no one capable of doing it, put all the *puṇḍit-s* in prison. When one day, Sage *Aṣṭāvakra* came to his court, he made the same request. The *Muni* (the Sage) agreed to do so provided the king qualified. Then he took the king along with his horse to a lonely spot in a forest, and told him to get up. The king put one foot in one stirrup, and before he could lift the second foot, the Sage said: "Stop, first you must accept me as your Guru." The King agreed. Then the *Muni* asked: "Where is the *Guru Dakṣinā*?" The King said: 'I place my body, mind, wealth, all my possessions at your feet.' The moment he said these words, he went into *samādhi* in that very posture, the second foot not yet lifted. A couple of days later, the Sage returned and recalled the king from his *samādhi* state. The king acknowledged gratefully that his doubt had been cleared.

When the body, mind and possessions are totally and unreservedly surrendered to the Guru, one gets absorbed in the Self. This is our real, natural state. The initiation into self-knowledge given by the Sage to the King is called *Aṣṭāvakra Gītā.*

58. THE SUN AND THE CLOUDS

Birth of bondage.

The sun is shining brightly in the sky. Suddenly dense dark clouds move across and hide the sun from view. The sky darkens. The sun is not manifest, but the clouds are. The day is cloudy and living beings are not happy. The clouds were formed by the sun itself, by its own heat, yet it is hidden by the clouds born of Sun itself!

In the same way, the Reality is shining all the time within us but we are not aware of it, because it is veiled from our vision by the clouds of *avidyā* (ignorance). The ego which has risen from the Self covers the Self and is fully manifest, as if it is the Reality. Then the ego says: "I alone am the Truth." From this, follows all the suffering which the ego projects. Because of these two effects of veiling and projection born out of ignorance of our true identity, we are in a state of bondage and limitation. When the cloud of ignorance is blown away, one has first-hand experience of the Reality which is ever shining, which in fact was never touched by the clouds.

[Source: V.C. 142-3]

59. THE SPARROW AND THE MIRROR

Mind alone creates its bondage

A large mirror was kept on the verandah of a house. A sparrow sat in front of it and happy to see another of his kind, went up to the mirror and pecked. The reflected sparrow also did the same. Excited by this response, the sparrow continued to peck; his beak began to bleed, but he would not stop. His mate called to him: "Come dear, let's fly out into the vast blue sky and be happy," but he did not hear her. The heavens beckoned him to freedom and bliss, but he was bound by the attachment which he himself had created, for his own reflection.

In the same way, the *jīva* gets bound to the world of sense objects. This bondage is created by the mind alone. In our ignorance and non comprehension of the Reality, we miss the real Bliss that is beckoning us.

Liberation comes only when this meaningless fascination for all that is not Self is got rid of (discarded). It is the mind itself that causes bondage, and it is the mind alone that liberates.

"*Mana eva manuṣyāṇām kāraṇam bandha-mokṣayoḥ*"

[Source: V.C. 173]

60. THE ROPE IN SNAKE

Projecting the Self on the not-Self is bondage.

A man is looking for a rope to tie a bundle. He sees a 'rope' under a tree and runs to pick it up. He is about to grab it, he gets the shock of his life when he discovers it to be a snake!

Similarly, we misunderstand the body to be the Self. And the consequences are as disastrous as grasping a snake - endless and meaningless travails of family, wealth, protection, preservation etc.. Holding on to the unreal, perishable, variable *anātma vastu* is the essence of bondage. In chasing the not-self, the Self - the unchanging, one without a second, is forgotten.

[Source: V.C. 138]

61. THE SILK-WORM

Wrong identification with not-Self is bondage

The silk-worm spins fine threads from its own saliva and weaves a cocoon around itself. The cocoon gets stronger and stronger, until at last the worm is truly trapped in the prison of its own making.

Similarly, once the identification that 'I am the body' has mistakenly arisen, this false notion weaves its own cocoon of demands for the preservation of the body.
These demands multiply and become so strong that the individual gets totally bound by them inescapably.. This is bondage - *saṁsāra duḥkham*. It arises out of *avidyā*, non-apprehension of our Real, Divine Nature.

[Source: V.C. 137]

62. THE LOAD-CARRIER

Bondage of the body.

A man who carries a load for a wage, longs for the time when he can reach his destination, so that he can off-load his burden. Then he puts down the load and is greatly relieved.

In the same way, this body is a burden to a man of discrimination. He looks forward to the time when he will be free from the bondage of the body, and be able to throw it away. When he sees another person dead, he looks forward to his own exit from the body.

[Source: L.F.R. 51]

63. THE BURNING WOOD

Bondage in the guise of freedom.

A log of wood burns and is left behind as fire. Salt disappears in the water and is left behind as salty taste.

In the same way, the thought (*ajñāna vṛtti*) that 'I am the body and therefore limited,' is destroyed and is replaced by a stronger thought (*tattva jñāna vrtti*) that "I am *sat-cit-ānanda svarūpa*". But this second knowledge is as much a bondage as the earlier *ajñāna*, as the individuality is still very much intact. It is still incorrect knowledge (*anyathā bodha*) gained through the medium of limitations. Correct knowledge (*yathā bodha*) is that where there is no knower-known difference.

This knowledge does not 'happen' ---- IT IS WHAT ONE ALWAYS IS.

[Source: A.A. III 9-10]

64. THE MAN WHO IMAGINED HE HAD BEEN IMPRISONED

Attention to the first person alone will reveal the non-existence of bondage and liberation.

A man was seen standing, facing a corner formed by two walls meeting each other at an angle. There was no third wall behind him. But he kept groping the two walls in front and wailing: 'Alas! I am imprisoned in this triangular room; how am I to free myself?'

A friend who observed this situation said: "Why don't you turn around to see if there is a way out?" The man did so and found that there was no third wall. So he said, 'Oh! there is no obstacle, let me escape this way.' The friend asked: "Why do you want to run away? If you don't run, will you be in prison?" The man laughed at himself: 'True, I was never imprisoned; it was only my delusion. Not looking behind was my bondage; finding no wall was my liberation. I am ever as I am.'

The two walls are the 2nd and 3rd persons. The first person is the absence of the third wall. Liberation can never be attained through the 2nd and 3rd persons; but only by attention to the first person - Who am I? This inquiry will lead to the knowledge that the ego is non-existent. The First Person is independent of the other two persons. Then the Truth is realized that both bondage and freedom are false.

[Source: The Path of Sri Ramana. I. pp. 133-4]

65. THE CHILD AND THE GOBLIN

Bondage and freedom have no meaning for the man of wisdom.

A mother had to struggle every day to feed her restless, playful child. So one day, she said: "Look son, there is a goblin waiting just round the corner. If you don't eat your meals properly, he will carry you away and gobble you up."

The child gulped down his food fast, watching for the goblin out of the corner of his eye. This ruse worked for a long time.

One day, the mother told the child: "The goblin is dead. He won't bother you anymore." The child jumped with joy, relieved that the goblin would no more frighten him. So, the mother made the non-existent goblin "die" in order to reassure the child. To her, the goblin never existed, and his "death" meant nothing.

Similarly, once the Self is realized, there is neither bondage nor freedom. Both are only projections of the mind.

[Adapted from: A.A. III. 13]

66. THE BIRD ON THE PERCH

The Self is always free.

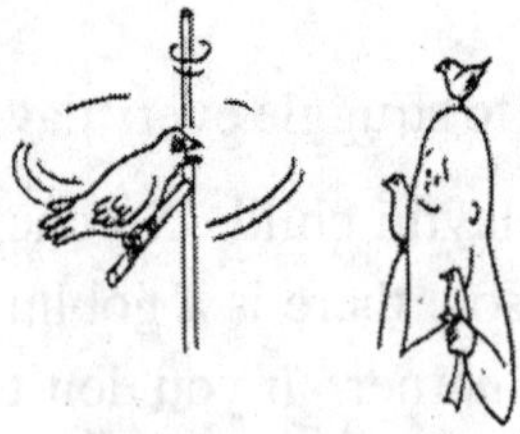

A bird is sitting on a rotating perch. It has the freedom to fly always but instead, it only grips the perch harder, and thus allows itself to be caught by the hunter.

Similarly, the Self is never in bondage. It is therefore meaningless to talk in terms of bondage and freedom. These are only concepts in relation to each other; a mental creation of the *jīva.* Like the sun knows neither light nor darkness, these are only in the human perception; the sun is beyond both.
Bondage is only in the mind. True Freedom (*mukti*) is freedom from the hallucination of being in bondage. The Supreme Bliss that the Self is, is beyond bondage and freedom.

"*Bandha mukti atītam parama sukham.*"

[V.S. 29]

67. THE QUARRELING COUPLE

Knowledge is as invalid as ignorance.

There was once a couple who were constantly arguing. One day they decided to change their roles, and therefore exchanged their heads.

And both died!

In the same way, the couple, *jñāna* and *ajñāna* always exist together, contradicting each other. When one tries to analyze *ajñāna* first, hoping that thereafter to analyse *jñāna,* they both disappear. The inquiry into the validity of ignorance negates the validity of knowledge.

[Source: A.A-VIII. 15]

68. THE MAN WHO WANTED TO CUT HIS OWN SHADOW

Ignorance exists in its own absence.

A man got annoyed with his shadow because it kept following him. He took a sword and tried to cut it. All he achieved was to hit the ground and cut some grass that was growing on it. The shadow remained whole and unharmed. It was impossible to harm the shadow because it was not an object of cognition. It did not exist!

In the same way, if one tries to destroy ignorance (the shadow) with the sword of the word, it will be just as futile. Ignorance cannot be removed because it does not exist. Mere intellectual study cannot lead to the Truth. The only way to get out of the entanglement of the world is to treat it like a shadow.

[Source: A.A. 24, 43-44]

69. THE CAMPHOR AND THE FIRE

Self-destruction of thought-knowledge is the genesis of Pure Knowledge.

Camphor comes in contact with fire during *ārati.* First the fire destroys the camphor, then the fire also dies, because it cannot exist without the presence of camphor.

So also, thought-knowledge destroys thought-ignorance, and then itself disappears. Out of those ashes rises Pure Knowlege.

[Source: A.A. IV. 5]

70. THE MAN WHO SETS HIS HOUSE ON FIRE

Knowledge destroys ignorance and then destroys itself.

A man locked himself in his house and then set the house on fire.

Along with the house, he was also destroyed.

In the same way, objective knowledge has existence only in ignorance. When the (house of) ignorance is destroyed, the knowledge is also destroyed. *Jñāna vṛtti* destroys *ajñāna vṛtti* and then gets destroyed itself. Thereafter, only Pure undifferentiated knowledge remains.

[Source: A.A. IV. 4]

71. THE KNIFE WHICH WANTED TO CUT ITSELF

Pure knowledge cannot be the "object" of knowledge.

A knife wants to cut itself. Is that possible? The cutting object is the knife, the object to be cut is also the same knife. The knife and its sharpness are not two.

In the same way, any attempt to objectify the Truth and "understand it" as an object of knowledge is impossible. Through *vṛtti jñānam* (thought-knowledge), *bheda* alone is established. Whereas, Pure Knowledge always goes back to its original state of equilibrium, where there is no knower of the knowledge.
This knowledge is gained by one who has the inner vision (*āvṛtta cakṣuh*).

[Source: A.A. IV. 3]

72. THE MOON AND ITS SEVENTEENTH *KALA*

In pure knowledge, there is neither knowledge nor ignorance.

On a full moon night, the complete moon is seen. On *amāvāsya* night, there is 'no moon'. In between only, segments of the moon are seen.

From the point of view of the moon - it is neither absent nor incomplete (the seventeenth *kalā*); the sixteen *kalā-s* (phases) do not exist. The full moon is *jñāna vṛtti*, the *amāvāsya* is *ajñāna vṛtti*.

In the same way, in Pure Knowledge, knowledge and ignorance do not exist. There is neither 'waxing' of *jñāna* nor 'waning' of *ajñāna*. There is Pure *(śuddha) Jñāna* alone. It is neither brightened by knowledge nor dulled by ignorance. This *śuddha jñāna* is our essential nature.

[Source: A.A. IV. 15-17]

73. THE MIRROR AND THE REFLECTED FACE

Pure knowledge is abiding in experience only.

I want to see my own face; so I hold a mirror in front to create a duality (where there is none). "I, the original face" enter the mirror and come out as "I, the Reflection". I know the reflected face is only myself. I am one without a second.

In the same way, in every experience, the enjoyer (I), the enjoyed (the reflection) and the enjoyment are one only, not three. This is what is sought in every experience - **the experiencing alone**, where there is neither the experiencer nor the experienced. THIS INTENSE LIVING IN THE EXPERIENCING IS MEDITATION. In such a place, there is knowledge without a knower. This undifferentiated knowledge, this one-ness, is the Reality.

[Source: A.A. IV. 2]

74. SUGAR AND ITS SWEETNESS

The Self is self-existing

The inherent nature of sugar is its sweetness. For its sweetness, it does not depend on any other object. On the other hand, it is able to lend its sweetness to other objects like milk, rice, etc., which have no sweetness of their own.

In the same way, the *ātma-tattva* which is of the nature of experience, does not depend on any other object for experience. It is beyond cause and effect, beyond the realm of intellectual understanding.
When the five *kośa-s* (sheaths) are negated, when there is nothing to experience objectively, the *Ātmā* continues to be. It is self-existing *(svayambhu)*. It is never denied.

Bodhātmā tu na hiyate

[Source: P.D. III. 14-15]

75. THE *NAIVEDYA* TO LORD *GANESHA*

Only the Self exists.

A devotee made an image of Lord *Gaṇeśa* out of jaggery, installed it and worshipped it. At the end, he pinched out a small amount of jaggery from the same image, and offered it as *naivedya* (offering).

In the same way, when we say that we offer our body, soul and possessions to the Lord, does any of these belong to us in the first place? Instead, it would be more truthful to say: "O Lord, I had falsely imagined that what indeed is yours, was mine. Now I realize that everything is yours alone. Nothing is mine." This knowledge that there is nothing but God or Self; that "I" and "mine" do not exist, that only Self exists, is *jñāna* (knowledge).

[Source: D.D.V. p. 42]

76. THE HOST AND HIS *ATITHI*

The Self is *cit-svarūpa* (of the nature of consciousness)

A devotee of the Lord had taken a vow that he would not eat his daily meal without feeding an *atithi*. Once it happened, that for two days, no guest turned up and he had to go without food. On the third day, a guest came to his door; he was overjoyed and received the guest with all respect and honour.

When the food was served, the guest began to eat without saying the customary prayers. The host got upset and admonished the guest: "What kind of *atithi* is he, who does not even offer thanks to the Lord for the daily bread? I don't like to serve such an *atithi*."

Thereupon, the guest got up and left. That night the Lord appeared in the host's dream and asked: "Whom should I thank? Myself? Can I do my own prayers?"

In the same way, when every being is I alone, the same consciousness, there is no one either to love or to hate. There is no inclusion or exclusion in the manifestation of completeness.
I am none other than the *cit-svarūpa* (consciousness)

[Source: B.A.-7]

77. THE GOLDEN ORNAMENT

Pure knowledge is *Brahman*

A lady takes a golden necklace to the goldsmith to be melted and made into another ornament. The goldsmith takes one look and returns it saying: "Madam, I deal only in gold; and this is no gold." The woman is shocked: "It was such a beautiful necklace. How could I have been deceived like this?"

"Simple Madam," says he: "Your attention was on the name and the form; mine is always on the gold only."

When the attention is on the world of names and forms, that understanding *(dhī)* is called *alaṅkāra buddhi;* when the attention is on the Pure Consciousness, because of which all the names and forms are possible, it is called *suvarṇa buddhi.*

From every object of knowledge, when the object is rejected, what remains is Pure knowledge which is not knowledge of something, but knowledge itself. That is *Brahman.*

[Source: P.D., III. 21]

78. THE CINEMA PICTURE ON THE SCREEN

The Self is all

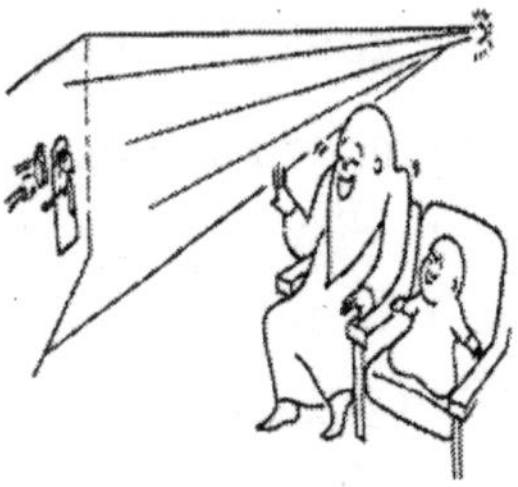

Scenes are projected on the screen in a cinema show. The pictures move; tragedies and comedies are enacted. We laugh with the comedies and weep with the tragedies. As seer, we pay attention only to the pictures and ignore the screen, the substratum, which is still, totally unaffected by the pictures, although they cannot exist without the screen.

Similarly, the Self is the screen on which activities are going on. Man is aware of the activities, but unaware of the Self. But he is not apart from the Self. Aware or not, the Self is universal, unmoving, unchanging. And the play of activities on this substratum will continue, but they do not alter or affect the substratum.

[Source: TWRM. 313]

79. THE IMAGE IN THE MIRROR

The self is all-pervading .

The reflection is in the mirror. The mirror pervades within the reflection as well as without. The reflection has no existence apart from the mirror. When the reflection is not there, the mirror continues to be.

Similarly, the Consciousness is reflected in the three bodies - the gross, the subtle and the causal. The reflection, the *ābhāsa*, is the *jīva*, the ego. But the Self is ever present, inside and outside the three bodies. With reference to a room or pot, we can call space within or without. Once the walls are pulled down, it is only one all-pervading space. So also on apprehending the Self, its all-pervading nature is experienced.

[Source: Ast.G. I. 19]

80. THE OBJECTS IN SPACE

Self cannot be negated

When objects are removed from a room, only space is left, which is formless and dimension-less. Space cannot be removed; only objects can be removed. Space is always left behind.

In the same way, when through discrimination (*viveka*), the *pañca kośa-s* are negated, the Self which supports the *kośa-s* is left behind. What is left un-negated and un-negatable is the *Ātmā*, the *satya svarūpa.*

"Śakyeṣu bādhiteṣuṣvānte śiṣyate yat tat eva tat."

[Source: P.D. III. 30]

81. THE *MUNJA* GRASS

The Self is unattached, action-less.

The *muñjā* grass has an empty core, enveloped by sheaths of leaves, like the stem of the banana tree. When the sheaths are removed one by one, and one reaches the central core, there is "nothing".

Similarly, the core of our Being, the Self, is unattached, action-less, free, totally uninfluenced by the layers of all that is perceived as the "seen".

Remove the sheaths of the perceptible, phenomenal world; layer after layer (*neti, neti, iti*) (it is not, it is not), and reach the core-the subject without an object-in the Heart. Once this objectless, unattached Awareness is realized, all the world of names and forms merge in it.

[Source: V.C. 153]

82. PLAY WITHIN A PLAY

The Self is ever-unchanging and unchangeable.

A play is being projected on a cinema screen. The scene shows a King sitting on his throne in the durbar hall. He is watching a play in which the artists depict various characters.

The King in the main play is the 'seer' and the play within that play is the 'seen' for that seer. Both the seer and the seen are only shadows on the same screen which is the only reality, supporting the pictures of the seer and the seen.

So also the "seer" - the ego, and the "seen" - the world, together constitute the mind, and the mind is supported by the Self. The mind with its dichotomy of seer and seen is only a superimposition on the Self.

To the seer, the Self seems changeful because it is identified with the mind. But the Self is ever the same, unchanging and unchangeable.

[D.D.V. p. 86]

83. THE OWL

Distinguishing the changeful from the changeless.

The owl sees in darkness. Darkness is its world of activity. In sunlight, it is blinded and sees nothing.

So also the world parades before ignorance, but disappears before right analysis. The world cannot stand the sunlight of investigation because of its changing unreal nature. One should constantly scrutinize the world and distinguish between the changeful objective phenomena and the changeless subjective consciousness, like the unchanging surface of the mirror, and the changing images in it.

[Source: T.U. XI]

84. THE DISCIPLE CROSSING THE RIVER

The association-less-one is the self.

By the Grace of his Guru, a disciple crossed the river of *saṁsāra.* On reaching the other shore, he looked back. The Guru was smiling, but there was no river.

One can cross something only if there is something to cross.

Similarly, the whole world, the *saṁsāra,* is like the *vandhya putra* (the son of a barren woman); it does not exist. It appears in its own non-existence.

Inquiry of Self thus leads to the discovery that neither the enjoyer, the *bhoktā,* nor the experiences have reality. All sufferings and enjoyments are born out of illusion. Ultimately, we are lead to discover our independent existence - the *kūṭastha,* the Pure Self. This is the only Reality.

[Source: P.D. vii. 198, B.U. 4.1.4]

85. THE KING IN THE DURBAR HALL

The Self is a mere witness to the play of matter.

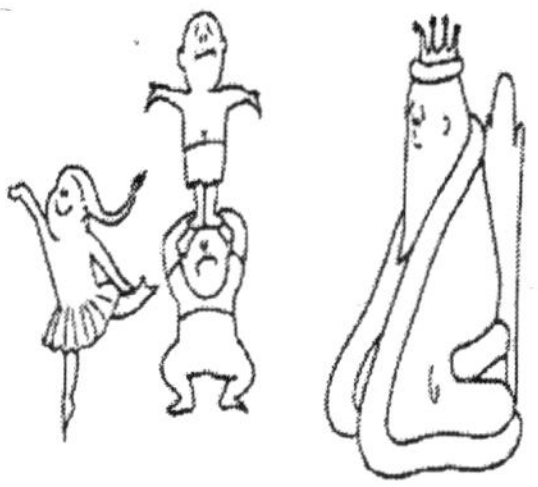

A King was sitting in the durbar hall watching all that was going on - a non-participating observer of the dance, the drama and the bustle happening in front of him. However, although he is disinterested, he is all-powerful.

In the same way, the Self is only a witness of the play of matter - the body, the senses, the mind, the intellect (the *prakṛti*). It stands aloof and does not identify Itself with what is going on in the entire cosmic order, nor does it identify itself with what is happening within us in the different layers of matter.

Atmānam Rājavat sadā

[Source: A.B. 18]

86. THE LIGHT IN THE THEATRE HALL

The Self is the witness of presence and absence.

The light is burning brightly in the theatre hall. It illuminates itself as well as the theatre, the audience and the actors. When the play is over, everyone leaves. But the light continues to shine and reveal the empty hall, the void.

In the same way, 'I,' the witness, lights up the ego, the intellect, the sense-objects, the three states of consciousness and the three periods of time. Even when all these cease to exist, I, the Self exists, as luminous as ever. The Self or that by which all modifications and their absence, the void, is perceived, is always present.

[Source: P.D. X]

87. THE HEN AND THE CHICKS

The Self is the support for all three states of consciousness.

A hen roams about all day long, but as dusk falls, she calls her chicks to her, enfolds them under her wings and goes to rest for the night.

So also, the subtle individual being, after gathering the impressions and experiences of the waking and dream states, enters with them into the causal body (deep sleep state) which is characterized by nescience (*avidyā*), the *tamo guṇa*. The experience in deep sleep is not true bliss. It is only the result of the negative aspect of such bliss, of the absence of thought. It is transitory. Such bliss is only *ābhāsa*, the counterfeit of Supreme Bliss. The reality is different from the three states. It is the basis, the support and witness of all the three experiences.

[Source: TWRM 617]

88. THE DIVER

The Self underlies all the experiences.

A diver plunges into the depths of the ocean to search for a long lost treasure. He finds the desired thing but cannot make his discovery known to the expectant persons on the shore, until he emerges from the water.

Similarly, the experience of bliss in deep sleep is a fact, but no one is able to recollect it. The sleeper cannot express his experience because he cannot contact the organs of expression until he is awakened by his *vāsanā-s* in due course.

The Self is the basis of all experiences, be they of the waking, dream and deep sleep states. It remains the witness and support of them all.

[Adapted form: TWRM. 617]

89. THE PERSON WHO WENT TO COLLECT *GANGA JALA*

***Paramātma tattva* is beyond time**

A person went on *tīrtha yātrā* (pilgrimage). The wide Ganga (Ganges) was flowing on and on infinitely. He collected the Ganga's water in a small copper pot. Out of that infinite Ganga, he could collect only a small finite pot of Ganga *jala.*

In the same way, Time is infinite because "I" am infinite. What passes through one *jīva*'s life-time is only a measured quantity of Time, with a beginning and an end.

But 'I,' the Self is 'nityam'(ever lasting); it is that which gives meaning to beginning and end, which is present both at the beginning and at the end, but is not influenced by either. It was not born nor will it ever die. It is never absent, it is ever present.

90. THE EYES TRYING TO SEE THEMSELVES

The *Ātma tattva* cannot reveal nor can be revealed.

The eyes are able to see everything outside where the seer and the seen are separate. But when they try to see themselves, they cannot; they can only remain still. The eyes are open, but there is no vision.

In the same way, in the *Ātma Tattva* which is one without a second, there is no place for the word to 'reveal' the Truth. In the Truth, there is neither a 'revealer' nor a 'revealed'. The visionless vision of the eyes is *Paramātmā* (Supreme Self). That which is eye of the eye, ear of the ear, speech of the speech is *Paramātmā.*

[Source: A.A. VI]

91. THE SON IN THE *GURUKULA*

The Self is hidden because of an obstacle.

Once a father visited a *pāṭhaśāla* where his son was studying. He stood outside the classroom where the children were chanting the *Veda-s*. He strained his ears to hear his son's voice, but in that collective chanting, he could not recognize it. The group chanting was the obstacle or *pratibandha* in singling out his son's voice, as it concealed his voice. Once the other children stopped chanting, then the son's voice became cognizable.

In the same way, the *Paramātma Tattva* which is of the nature of *Sat-Cit-Ānanda* (Existence, Consciousness, Bliss), is abundantly present but we are not able to know and experience it because of the contrary knowledge that deludes us. The remedy is to remove the obstacle which is veiling this essential nature, the Self.

[Source: P.D. I 12-14]

92. THE MAN AND HIS SHADOW

The tragedy of identifying with the not-self.

A man in hallucination thinks, he is his own shadow. Hence starts all his miseries: He finds his shadow lying on the road, all the traffic running over it most callously; at times the head of the shadow is in a filthy ditch or is being knocked against a tree. Thus all the suffering of the shadow becomes his. The only remedy lies in coming out of the hallucination and realizing his own Self.

In the same way, all our sorrows arise because I, the *Ātman* (the self) misunderstand myself to be the shadow, the *anātman* (the not-self). This is the beginning of all bondages and limitations, all created by ourselves for ourselves.

"*Atra anātmā aham iti matih bandhaḥ.*"

To re-remember our true identity as the Pure Self is to end the tragedies that result from mis-apprehension of our real nature.

[Source: V.C. 137]

93. THE SON WHO WAS ADMONISHED

Contrary identity is an obstacle to the seeker.

A son was admonished by his father. The son did not like it, and mistook the father to be his enemy.

The essential nature of the father is his concern for the well-being of his child. But the child rejects this because he has come under the influence of unwanted factors. Therefore, the father is erroneously understood to be the opposite of what he really is.

In the same way, the Self is other than the body, mind etc., and the world is an illusion. But due to mistaken contrary identity, the Self is taken to be the body, mind etc., and the world is taken to be real. This is called *viparīta bhāvanā* (opposite understanding). It is a great obstacle in *Brahmābhyāsa* (practise of the Self). Single-pointed inquiry and contemplation will alone help in negating this erroneous notion and in establishing oneself in the twin thoughts: 'I' am other than this body; the world is *mithyā* (false). Let this be constantly contemplated upon (*Aniśam bhāvayet*)

[Source: P.D. VII. 109, 112]

94. THE STICK ON THE RIVER

False relationship - the cause of sorrow

A man standing on a river bank saw a walking stick with a silver handle floating down the river. He jumped into the water and swam after it. Just as he was about to grasp it, a strong current carried it away out of his reach. As he helplessly watched it being swiftly swept away, he bemoaned: "Oh, I have lost my cane."

The stick was no more his than of any other on the river bank. It was his desire to possess it that created a relationship between himself and the stick. This non-existent relationship born out of his ignorance gave the stick the potency to cause grief in him.

Our nature is happiness, but we surrender it by giving undue value to external things. And thus we make ourselves vulnerable to their tyranny. Devaluing the outer world of objects can be achieved only by recognizing the value of that Eternal Source of Bliss within us.

95. THE "RUNNING MOON"

Superimposing attributes on the attributeless-Self.

A child is looking up at the moon, thousands of miles away. A mass of clouds which are a couple of miles above him, move across the sky in front of the moon. "Oh, the clouds have 'covered' the moon," he explains. Presently, the moon emerges and to the child's imagination, it looks as if the moon is 'running away' from the clouds.

In the same way, the Self seems to act but participates in none of the activities of the *pañca kośa-s* (five sheaths). It has no agitation. It is steady, firm and dispassionate. But when the mind is agitated, it seems as if the Self is agitated. Thus the eruptions of the different layers of matter are wrongly superimposed on the Glorious Self. **To experience the Self without the intervention of matter sheaths is to realize its infinitude.**

[Source: A.B. 19]

96. THE TRAVELLER AND THE GHOST

Superimposition of the pluralistic world on the Truth.

A weary traveller was trudging along a dark road. Suddenly he was startled by the vision of a huge ghost with head, arms and legs. He rubbed his eyes and looked again and was much relieved to discover that it was only the stump of an old dead tree. In that moment of cognition, the ghost vision of many parts rolled away and only the reality of one tree stump remained. The ghost had been only where the stump was. In fact, the ghost arose from substratum of the stump, borrowed pseudo-reality from it and merged back into it.

In the same way, on the Supreme - the only Reality, the mind superimposes the plurality of the phenomenal world. When by discrimination, the world of names and forms is transcended, all the superimposition rolls away, and the Eternal Blissful, substratum is revealed in its Fullness (*Pūrṇatva*).

[Source: I.U. Mantra.]

97. THE PAINTED WALL

Superimposition of *māyā* (illusion) on *Brahman* (the all-pervading Self).

An artist has painted a huge mural on a wall. The colour coatings on the wall have created many scenes and figures which were all only imaginary and which covered the wall itself.

In the same way, *māyā* superimposed on the Brahman creates a multitude of illusory names and forms which cover the Brahman itself - the very support of these names and forms.

[Source: P.D. II 59]

98. THE TANK COVERED BY MOSS

The Self is covered by its own *māyā śakti* (power of illusion).

A beautiful tank in a temple is not often used. Its surface is completely covered by a green sheet of moss, born out of the water itself. The water beneath cannot be seen nor is the sun's reflection visible. When the moss is pushed aside, the clear water is seen, in which the brilliant reflection of the sun is revealed.

As soon as the hand is lifted, the moss quickly moves over to cover the water surface again. The water and the sun's reflection are once again hidden from view.

In the same way, the Self is covered by our identity with the moss of the *pañca kośā*-s (five sheaths), which is born of the Self itself, by its own power of projection (*Māyā Śakti*). Because of this covering of wrong perceptions, the mind is not clear and cannot reflect the sun of Divinity. Remove the moss of ego-centric desires, turn the mind inwards. The ever present consciousness will be reflected in the clear waters of the mind. Be ever vigilant, as otherwise the moss of *Māyā* (illusion) will return and cover the Self again by delusion. Let streams of study and reflection wash out the moss which obstructs the vision.

[Source: V.C. 149-150]

99. THE STUDENT WHO WANTED *BRAHMOPADESHA* (Advice on the Supreme Self)

The two sins that beset a seeker.

A student approached a Master and asked for *Brahmopadeśa.* The Master said: "*Bhagavān* (Lord), you are yourself *Paramātmā* (supreme Self)."

The student thought that the Master was poking fun at him, and so he went to another Master who also gave him the same *upadeśa* (advice). Seeing the student looking unconvinced, he put him to work in the *āśrama* cowshed for twelve years. At the end of it, the *Mahātmā* gave him the *upadeśa*: "*Tat Tvam Asi* (Thou art That)".

The student asked: 'Why did you not say so at the beginning? Why did you have to put me through this long travail?' The Master said: "I did tell you so, but your understanding that time was that *Paramātmā* was far away and that you were a limited being."

In the same way, the two sins that beset a seeker are (a) that he is a limited being, under the tyranny of several limitations (*parichinnatā*) and (b) that the *Paramātmā* is separate from him in time, space and object, (*parokṣatā*), whereas He is here, now, and in every situation.

[Source: B.A. 10]

100. THE BIRTH AND DEATH OF THE THUNDERSTORM

Self knowledge alone can remove ignorance.

The sky is clear and bright. All of a sudden, clouds gather as if from nowhere. The sky darkens, lightning and thunder arise; the Lord sends down torrential rains as if for the fun of it. When strong winds blow, the clouds are dispelled, the darkness is lifted, the downpour ends, and tranquility prevails again.

In the same way, in the clear sky of *Sat-Cit-Ānanda* (Existence-Consciousness-Bliss) appear the clouds of *māyā* (illusion). The mind flashes lightning in the form of dream and waking states. The loud thunder of "I - am - the body" ego-sense drowns all words of wisdom. This ignorance plunges the *jīva* (living unit) into the torrential rains of the cycle of birth and death, creation and dissolution. All of us want to escape from this whirlpool of *karmā* (action). There is only one way - the strong winds of Self-inquiry should disperse the clouds, stop the rains. Then the plurality ends. There is no more bondage nor liberation. Only the tranquil Self remains. This is the final fulfilment.

[Source: *Sadācāra*: 40-1]

101. THE HUNGRY DREAMER

Awakening to Reality is only through the illusory experience of the waking world.

A man dreamt that he was ravishingly hungry. He was expecting food to be served by his dream-wife; but before it could arrive, he woke up.

He demanded of his wife: "Why did you not hurry up? I was so hungry in my dream!" His wife retorted: "Ask your dream-wife. She should know!"

Dream hunger can be satisfied only by dream food. In the same way, although the knowledge gained in the waking world is not real knowledge, this illusory knowledge alone can help us in coming out of the illusion-the *saṁsāra* that the world is. The illusory nature of the *saṁsāra* can be known only by analyzing the illusory experiences. There is no other way.

[Adapted from P.D. VIII. 17]

102. THE HUNGRY MAN AT A FEAST

Inquiry into the Self -- only *sādhanā* (disciplined pursuit) to the Truth.

A hungry man sees many people eating a hearty feast. But his hunger is not satiated by their eating. Only when he is invited in, and is fed sumptuously, is his hunger appeased.

In the same way, by going round and round, asking innumerable questions about happiness, and all the time forgetting one's own Self, one gets nowhere. It is wasted effort. There will be *śānti* (peace) only if one inquires about one's own Self. Then no other question will arise and one finds the Truth.

[Source: LSR. I. 50]

103. THE SAGE AND THE KING "ON" THE ELEPHANT

Self-enquiry is to focus the mind at its source.

Ribhu, the great sage, had taught his disciple, *Nidagha*, the Supreme Truth. Although *Nidagha* could not shake off his addiction to ceremonial religion (the *karma kāṇḍa*), the sage would periodically visit him to instruct him. Once he went to the city where *Nidagha* lived, disguised as a village rustic. He found his disciple watching a procession. "What is the bustle about?", he asked. 'The King is coming in a procession.' "Where is the King?", the sage asked. 'It is he who is seated on the elephant,' came the reply. The sage said: "Yes, I see too, but who is the King and which is the elephant?" *Nidagha* grew impatient, 'Don't you know this? The King is above, and the elephant is below.' The rustic (sage) pleaded, "Please, what is the meaning of above and below?" *Nidagha* lost his cool, 'Alright, bend down. I will show you.' The sage bent down, and *Nidagha* jumped on him and said, 'Now do you understand, you are below and I am above.' The sage persisted, "I see, but which of us is You, and which 'I'?!" At this question, *Nidagha* recognized his *Guru* and fell at his feet...

There are no separate entities as You and I in Pure Consciousness. The aim is to transcend here and now the superficialities of physical existence through *Ātma vicāra* (reflection on the Self). When one turns the mind within and seeks the source of thought, where is "You" and where is "I"!

[Source: *Viṣṇupurāṇa* II. XVX XVI]

104. THE SALT DOLL

Self -knowledge leads to annihilation of individuality.

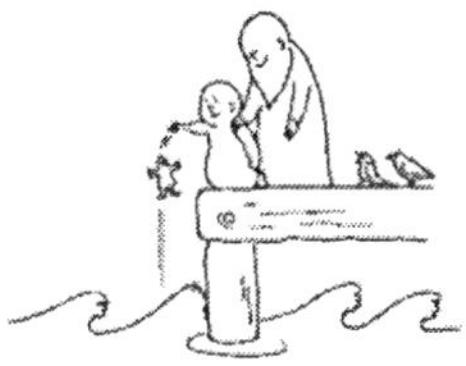

A salt-doll wanted to find out the depth of the ocean. So it jumped into the sea, only to disappear and to become one with the ocean. There was no doll, and no effort to measure the depth.

In the same way, when the *buddhi* (the individuality), in its arrogance wants to investigate about the *Paramātmā* (Supreme Self), the individuality disappears. There is no one to come back and report. Starting out to establish the validity of *dvaita* (duality), one ends up discovering the non-dual Truth. One disappears in one's own inquiry. It is an experience without an experiencer.

[Source: A.A. I.9]

105. *NARAYANA*

Self-enquiry leads to self-annihilation

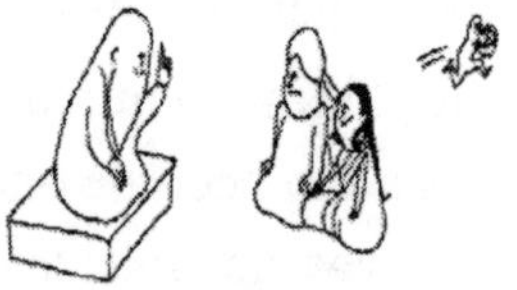

Nārāyaṇā appeared from nowhere at a marriage function and made himself indispensable, that he gained the confidence of both sides. Each side thought he belonged to the other. After the wedding was over, both sides looked out for him to thank him. On enquiry, they discovered that he belonged to neither side, that he was a super-con man who had made away with their valuables and vanished.

In the same way, the ego borrows the dynamism from the Consciousness, and the inertia from the *prakṛti* (matter), and starts appearing sometimes on the bridegroom's (consciousness) side, sometimes on the bride's (*prakṛti*) side. When inquiry is made into the nature of this "I," the ego, the subject "I" itself disappears.

Aham ayaṁ kuto bhavati cinvataḥ
Ayi patati ahaṁ nija vicāraṇam

[U.S. 19]

106. THE GOOSE-BERRY ON THE PALM OF ONE'S HAND

To know the Self, only the Self is needed.

A man was holding something in his hand. His friend asked: "What have you got in your hand?" In reply, he held out his hand and opened it. On his palm, lay a big, ripe *āmalaka* (gooseberry) fruit. With its rich translucency, it was vividly recognizable.

When something is self-evident, it is customary to compare it with *hastāmalaka.* However, even here, to know that it is an *āmalaka* fruit, a hand is needed, a palm that will and can feel a fruit on it, an eye that can see, and a person who already knows what fruit it is, etc. etc. But the Self is so self-evident that for knowing it, nothing at all is needed ... except the Self.

First, one see the Self as objects, then sees the Self as void (absence of objects; then one sees the Self as Self. In this last, there is no seeing, because seeing is being.

[Source: D.D.V.]

107. THE PEARL-DIVER

Steadfastness in Self-attention

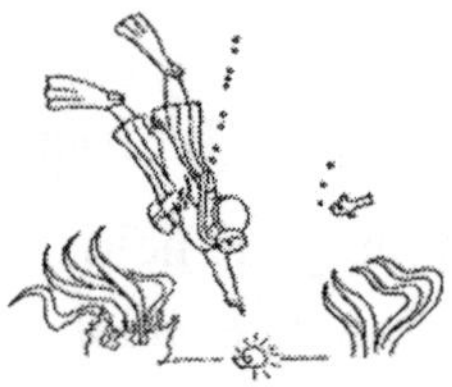

The pearl-diver ties a stone to his waist, dives ito the sea with just one single purpose and picks up the pearls lying at the bottom.

In the same way, the seeker tying the stone of *vairagya* (dispassion i.e. not attending to second or third persons), should dive deep within himself (the first person), and attain the pearl of the Self. He resorts to only one uninterrupted Self-remembrance (*sva-svarūpa-smaraṇam*), until he attains the goal-the Self.

[Source: The Path of Sri Ramana I - App. I]

108. A MAN WHO DIGS A WELL

Seek till you find

A man begins to dig a well. He rejects all the dirt, the clay, the gravel, the stones, in short, all that is not water till he reaches water - the life giving spring.

In the same way, give your heart and mind in digging into yourself-- to brooding over "I AM": What is I , how is it, what is its source, its life, its meaning...till you discover the True Self.

[Adapted from: NDM: in I am That.]

109. THE STUDIOUS STUDENT

Brahma jñāna (Supreme Knowledge) is never lost.

A student studies hard all during the day. Whatever he has studied is forgotten in the dream and deep sleep states. But when he wakes up the next morning, what he had studied is not forgotten.

In the same way, once the Supreme knowledge--*Brahma jñāna* is gained by *vedānta vicāra*, it can never again be lost. It leads to firm abidance in the Self.

[Source: P.D. II. 107]

110. THE COTTON AND THE SUN

Self is Accessible only to the extremely subtle mind.

In the sunshine, cotton does not burn. But if the same sun's rays, when made to pass through a lens and converge on the cotton, the cotton catches fire.

In the same way, the awareness of the Self is present at all times, but it is not inimical to ignorance, it cannot destroy ignorance. However, in the moments of deep meditation, the subtle state of thought is grasped, then ignorance is destroyed. Therefore, fix the attention on the Pure I after the subsidence of all thoughts. Then hold on to it. It is no other than the Real Self, which is of extraordinary subtlety.

"*Ativa suksmam paramatma tattvam*"

[Sources: TWRM. 624, V.C. 361]

111. THE LADY WHO LOST HER ORNAMENT

Re-discovery of the Ever-Realized Self

A woman thought she had lost her necklace, and started searching for it everywhere. She enquired of her friends if they had seen it. At last one kind friend pointed out: "Why, it is there on your neck!" The woman felt the necklace around her neck and was overjoyed that it had been "found". Her happiness in "re-discovering" it was the same as if it had really been lost, and recovered. In fact she had never 'lost' it, nor had she 'recovered' it. Yet she was once miserable, and now was happy.

So also, the Self is always realized, only now it is obscured. When the veil of ignorance is removed, one feels the joy of re-discovery of the ever-realized Self. The ever-present realization appears to be a new realization. It is a gain of that which is already gained. As the eagerness for true knowledge grows, the wrong knowledge diminishes in strength until it disappears.

[Adapted from TWRM. 490]

112. THE PANDURANGA BHAJAN

The Self Always is ... in its Natural Place

The *Pāṇḍuranga Bhajan* begins in the first quarter of the night. Devotees with tinkling anklets go round and round a central lamp-stand, singing: "Panḍharpur is thus far, Panḍharpur is thus far, come, let's go."

They do not go even one step forward, but continue going round and round ... As the third quarter is reached, they sing: "See, there is Pandharpur! Here is Pandharpur, see, see ..."

At dawn, they still go round and round, in the same circle round the same lamp, at the same distance; but now they sing: "We have arrived at Panḍharpur. This is Pandharpur..." and they salute the lamp-stand.

In the same way, we go round and round the *ātmā*, saying: "Where is *Ātma*, where is it? Until the dawn of *jñāna dṛṣṭi* is reached. Then we say: "This is *Ātmā*, This is me, the true state is always there; at all times."

[Source: LSR. 83]

113. THE *SVAYAMVARA* (Self choice of a Groom)

"You are Yourself"

A King held a big *svayamvara* for his beautiful daughter. The princess walked slowly down the rows of eligible princes seated expectantly. As her maid described the details of each bachelor, the princess paused, listened attentively ... and passed on as if communicating, "No, not this one," until she was in front of the man of her choice. Then, she stood still, looked down, and remained silent.

So also, *Vedānta* tells you, "You are not the body, not the mind, nor the intellect, nor the ego, nor anything that you can think of." Find out who you are. Silence denotes that: "You are Yourself" -- the Self, that is to be found out by oneself.

[Source: T.W.R.M. 620]

114. THE NEWLY ORDAINED *SANYASI*

Awakening to One's Real Nature

Ramaṇa was recently ordained as a monk. He was given a new name and new ochre robes, and his head was shaved.

Soon after, as he was walking through a village, someone accosted him: "Baba, Baba..." He did not respond, but walked on.

He had lived as Ramaṇa for so many years, that even though he had gone through an elaborate *dīkṣā* (instruction) ritual, he had not yet forgotten his man identity. It would take him time to get firmly established in his *swāmi* (master of the Self) identity.

In the same way, the *jīva* has been bound by this strong rope of body identification for countless number of lives. It has to be cut asunder with the sharp sword of Self-knowledge: "I am consciousness."

[Source: Asht.G. 14]

115. THE ONE WHO LOST HIMSELF

The Self is neither lost nor gained

A person was with himself. Forgetting this, he loses himself. And goes searching for himself for a long time. Then he remembers himself, and discovers that the one he was searching for, and himself are one and the same! Would he be elated?

Similarly, would the self-effulgent, ever-present Self celebrate that it has gained itself?! To do so would not be true knowledge, because it would be in the realm of relative thought. **That is only bondage.**

[Source: A.A. III. 22]

116. THE MAN WHO HAD "NO ROOM" IN HIS HOUSE

Finding the Self in the Heart.

A man had a big house. But all of the room was filled with junk. Then he complained that he had no room for himself (for his own body)!

In the same way, we fill the mind with false ideas, unnecessary *vāsanā-s*, and then complain that there is no room in the Heart for the Self. If all the wrong impressions are swept out, what remains is a feeling of plenty. And that is the Self. There will be no separate "I". It is a state of egoless-ness. Instead of seeking the Self, to say "no room, no room", is like shutting the windows and saying, "no sun, no sun". In the emptying of the heart, the Self is filled fully.

[Source: LSR II. 4]

117. THE LAMP KEPT BETWEEN TWO ROOMS

The Self Alone Reminds the Self About the Self

A lamp is kept between two rooms, in the expectation that it will illumine both the rooms. But it does not. Neither is the darkness removed in the two rooms, nor are they filled with light.

So also in the Self, by taking the support or *alambana* of the word (i.e. what is available through speech), neither is ignorance removed nor is the Self realized. To have the experience of immortal being, one must have the courage to drop all supports including the word, on which we have been leaning heavily for so long.

The eye does not go there (To the Truth), nor speech, nor mind ... [Ke. U. I. 3] The Self is *sva-samvedya*-self-knowing. There is no need for anything other than the Self to remind the Self about the Self.

[Source: A.A. VI]

118. THE STONE SEEKING ITS SOURCE

Merging in Self

A stone is thrown up into the air. It has left its source, the ground and has gone up. How far up, how long? Not forever. After reaching a certain height determined by the force of propulsion which separated it from its source, it tries to come down. It is continuous motion until it regains its source, where it is at rest.

Wherever there is a sense of separation, there is agitation and movement until that sense of separation is removed. So it is with us. So long as we have identified with the body, we are separate from the True Self. To drop this false identity is to regain our source. Then we are at peace, and happy. **Seek your source, merge in Self, and remain....all alone.**

119. THE DEER THAT RESTED

The State of Being

A deer is taking rest in the shadow of a tree. The colour of the shadow is neither light nor very dark, but half-way. It is the borderland. Deep blue, like clouds. That is that state.

That deep, dark blue state, that is the Grace of the *sadguru* (enlightened teacher). Everything flows out of that state; but this principle does not claim anything, is not involved in anything coming out of it.
This is the state of the *Jñānī* (knower), a very rare *samādhi* (absorption) state, the most natural state, the highest state.

[Source: N.D.M. Prior to Consciousness, p. 8]

120. THE THORN IN THE FOOT

The State of Self-hood

A man is walking through a jungle, when a thorn enters his foot. He stops, breaks off a long, straight thorn from a nearby bush, removes the thorn lodged in his foot with it, then tosses both away, leaving only the foot!

In the same way, the *jñāna vṛtti* (knowledge-thought), removes the *ajñāna vṛtti* and gets diluted itself, and only the Pure Self remains. The illusory thought that, "I am the body" is replaced by *Aham Brahmāsmi* - "I am the Self"- thought. Ultimately, even this *akhaṇḍakāra aham Brahmāsmi vṛtti* also has to be discarded. What remains thereafter is *Samādāna* - the natural state of Self-hood.

Jñānājñāne parityajya jñānameva avaśiṣyate

[Source: *Sadācāra*. 5]

121. THE SAINT WHO PUT HIS HAND IN THE FIRE

Dis-Identification from the Body

One winter day, the saint of *Śirdi* was sitting before the *dhuni* (the eternal fire), pushing firewood into it now and again. Suddenly, instead of pushing a piece of wood, he thrust his arm into the fire. He came to his senses only when his devotees pulled him back. He explained: "A blacksmith's wife in some distant place got up in a hurry, and the baby on her lap fell into the fire. So I pulled the infant out and saved it."

Pain is only a movement in consciousness. The knower of consciousness cannot feel any pain. It is only when consciousness identifies with the body, that the body feels pain. As this identification lessens, the pain also becomes less and less, to a degree that with complete dis-identification with the body, one can put the hand in the fire, and not feel the pain! The effect of the fire will doubtless be there, but not the pain. Most pain and suffering is like this. If you pay attention, it is provoked, and you have to pamper it. If you don't pay attention and ignore the symptoms, they get lost.

[Sources: S.S.S.C, NDM. Prior to Consciousness, p. 15]

122. THE MAN WHO WAS TOLD HE WOULD DIE

Liquidating identity with body-mind.

A person met a man who gave him something to drink. Then he told the person: "I had put poison in that drink. You will die in six months."

The person got much frightened inthe belief that he would die in six months. Later he met a friend and told him what happened. The friend said: "Don't worry. Take this drink. There will be no death for you." The person drank it and felt relieved of his anxiety.

In the same way, we wander endlessly between concepts, ideas and creations of the mind, tossed to and fro between anxieties, fears and joys. Being thus caught in the flow of *Māyā* (illusion), there is nothing but misery. Instead, liquidate your identity with the body-mind. Be still in your being-ness.

[Source: NDM, Prior to Consciousness, p. 21]

123. THE FOOLISH MAN AND THE REFLECTED SUN

Realizing the Truth in the Self by turning away from body, mind, intellect

A foolish person saw the sun's reflection in a bucket of water and exclaimed: "Oh! Look, the sun has fallen into the bucket." A wise man passing by, ignored the bucket, the water and the reflection, and looked and saw the Self-luminous sun.

In the same way, the ignorant person identifies himself with the reflected consciousness (*adābhāsa*) and believes this to be his own identity.

But the wise man realized the Self-effulgent Reality (the sun) which illumines the body (the bucket), the water (the thoughts) and the reflected sun (the ego). These three are only *taṭastha lakṣaṇa-s*, symbols which help us to lift our vision high above these pointers to see the Self (the sun).

Therefore, turn away from the body, the intellect, and the reflected consciousness, contemplate in the heart-cave, the witness, the Self, the Knowledge Absolute, and realize the Supreme Reality.

[Source: V.C. 218-219]

124. THE BUSINESSMAN WHO SET UP A SHOP

The body should be utilized for the greatest profit: Self-Knowledge

A young businessman rented a shop. At first, he earned less than what he needed to pay as rent. He wondered if it was worthwhile to continue the business.

Then by more effort, he made just enough profit to pay the rent. His friend asked: "What kind of business are you running? It is worthwhile only if you make a profit of at least ten times the rent that you have to pay."

In the same way, we have rented this body for realizing the Self. The food, clothing, shelter is the rent we pay, using the mind, body and speech as instruments. If we do not pay the rent, we cannot live in this body, and earn the profit of Self-Realization. Nor can we afford to spend all our time and effort only to pay the rent. To do so would be like the businessman who earned only to pay the rent. The sincere seeker should be able to spend just a small portion of his time and energy for maintaining the body, so that he can devote all the remaining time to earn the greatest profit of Self-Knowledge.

[Source: The Path of Sri Ramana. I. App. 3]

125. THE TWO TRAVELLERS

Enduring life's experiences with equipoise.

Two persons were walking along the same path to reach a shrine. The path was narrow and steep, and both got equally tired. One knew that the destination was near; he put in a little extra effort, walked with determination, and reached the shrine. The other, not knowing that the destination was near, and lacking perseverance, succumbed to his fatigue and gave up.

Prārabdha karma (destiny) is the same for the wise man and the ignorant; but the response to it is different. The wise man endures his *prārabdha* with equanimity and courage. He is a *divya puruṣa* (illumined being). The ignorant man becomes discouraged *(dīnadhiḥ)* and uninspired.

[Source: P.D. VII. 133]

126. THE CRYSTAL AND THE HIBISCUS

Dis-identification from Thought-Disturbances.

The crystal by itself is colourless and clear. But when it is placed in front of a hibiscus flower, it appears red. Similarly, it takes on different hues depending on the object which is near it. Each object is an *upādhi* (object), that in the presence of which another object (the crystal), the *upahitam,* gets a false appearance. When the *upādhi,* the flower is removed, the crystal shines once again in its original purity.

Similarly, the Self is changeless, formless, crystal clear. It is pure *Cit.* Every thought is an *upādhi.* With every changing thought, "I" also seems to change, "I" takes on another personality. The *Cit* becomes *Citta* with every superimposition of thought, with such constantly changing stream of thoughts of family, friends etc.. 'I' am ultimately confused as to what my real nature is. Let us remember our true identity--the crystal, the Pure Self. Let us not identify ourselves with the *upādhi-s,* the thought disturbances. Let us remain tranquil - *praśāntam.*

[Sources: Kai.U., V.D., TWRM]

127. THE *RISHI* WITH THE CROOKED BODY

Overcoming the limitations of matter.

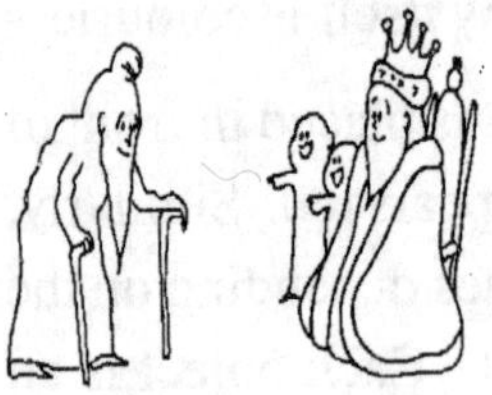

When *Aṣṭāvakra Ṛṣi* appeared in King *Janakā*'s court, the people gathered there, laughed at his crooked appearance. (His body had eight distortions.)

The *Ṛṣi* remarked, "Oh King, I thought that only wise people gather in your court, but I find only cobblers here whose vision is only on the skin ...!"

In the same way, when the attention is on the *upādhi-s* (object), one is buried at the level of matter alone. Importance is given to unimportant things like *varṇa* and *āśrama*, young and old, handsome or ugly, man or woman etc.. This is the *pravṛtti mārga* (path of involvement) born out of *avidyā* (ignorance). It has limited existence.

But the true seekers follow the *nivṛtti mārga* (path of withdrawal), where the criteria for classification is the level of Consciousness that is expressing through the individual. This path leads to the Abode of Unlimited Existence.

128. THE LOGS ON THE LAKE

Disidentify from relationships to identify with Self.

Logs of wood are floating on a lake. Two logs come together when the wind blows. The same wind blows and moves them apart a little later.

In the same way, the wind *(prārabdha)* (destiny), brings people together in relationships, the same *prārabdha* also breaks the relationships. No two,---be they husband-wife, father-son,---came into life together, and no two, departed together. He who would seek *Brahman* must transcend limitations of relationships. This is done by cutting off *rāga* (attachment) by remembering the transience of relationships, and by cutting off *dveṣa* (aversion) by accepting differences. Relationships invoke the individuality, the *ahaṁkāra* (the ego-ness). *Ahaṁkāra* limits; *Brahman* is limitless. Being free from relationships is being *atyāśramasthaḥ*.

129. THE MAN AND HIS REFLECTION

The Self is untouched by modifications.

A person standing on the shore of a lake sees his reflection upside down. But he ignores the inversion and comes to identify the reflection with himself. None of the distortions that happen to the reflection disturb him.

In the same way, a seeker ignores the joys and sorrows, and the names and forms, as having no validity. He knows that the real Self is the *Paramātma Tattva* (the supreme Self), the *Brahman*, which is untouched by any of the modifications.

[Source: P.D. XIII. 95]

130. THE WHEAT GRINDING

Citta Śuddhi (Purity of mind), the first step to Self-Knowledge

There lived in Śirdi a great Saint. He used tc grind wheat everyday in a hand-mill. The two stones of his mill were: *kārma* (action) - the lower, and *bhakti* (devotion) - the upper. The handle with which He worked the mill was *jñāna* (knowledge). The grain which he put into the mill were the sins, afflictions and miseries of the devotees.

Knowledge or Self-Realization is not possible unless there is the prior act of grinding of all our impulses, desires, sins of the three *guṇa-s*, and the *ahaṁkāra* which is so subtle that it is difficult to be got rid of.

Ātmānamaraṇiṁ kṛtvā praṇava cottarāraṇiṁ
Jñananirmathanābhyāsāt pāśaṁ dahati puṇḍitaḥ

[Kai. U. 11]

Making the ego the lower *araṇi*, *Oṁ* the upper *araṇi*, by churning with the path of Knowledge, the wise man burns up the cords of bondage.

[Source: S.S.S.C.]

131. THE MAN WHO IS SLEEPING IN A LONELY PLACE

Erasing the faculty of Knowingness.

A man is sleeping in a secluded place. He does not know himself that he is sleeping. The waker is also absent. Then, who will know?

In the same way, Pure Existence is beyond the limitation of existence and non-existence, beyond *sukha* (happiness) and *duḥkha* (unhappiness). Only when the faculty of "Knowingness" is born, do problems arise. Spiritual *sādhanā* (pursuit) is to erase this knowing-ness and be a mere witness to the thoughts. This is the state of being in "conscious sleep," where there is no differentiation of knower and known.

[Source: A.A - IV. 33-4]

132. THE TRAVELLER WHO LOST HIS WAY

Knowledge of Self destroys concepts of 'I' and 'Mine'.

A man arriving in a strange city at dusk lost his bearings, and did not know in which direction he was moving. On enquiring, a local resident pointed out the North by means of the Pole star. From this indication, the traveller was able to get his ignorance removed about the other three directions. This is because the other three directions have a definite relationship with the one known direction.

Similarly, once the Self is known as the one Universal Reality, (*tattva svarūpa*), we can immediately understand our true relationship with the world of objects on the one hand, and with our own matter envelopments, on the other. We gain a more balanced vision of our position in the scheme of things. Thereafter, concepts of 'I' and 'Mine' become meaningless.

"*Aham mama iti ca jñānam*
Bādhate digbramādivat."

[Source: A.B. 46]

133. *DRAUPADI'S* REFUGE IN KRISHNA

Transcending limitations of time and space
or
Paramātmā (Supreme Reality) is the closest of the close.

Draupadi called out to Lord *Kṛṣṇa* for help: "O *Dvārakāpurivāsī* (Inhabitant of Dwarikapuri)!"

There was no response, as if *Kṛṣṇa* said: "If I am *here* so far away, how can I come *there* and *now*?"

Then she calls out, *"Govinda"* (the one who is behind the sense organs, the one who is the support of all our faculties).

He appeared instantly and saved her.

Only when the limitations of time, space and object are transcended, does the Truth reveal itself.

[Source: B.A. 10-11]

134. THE PILGRIM WHO WANTED TO VISIT THE ABODE OF LORD VISHVANATH

"I am the beginning and the end."

A pilgrim from the South reached a city in the dead of night. He did not know where he was. He asked someone: "I want to go to *Vāraṇasi* (Benaras) and have *darśana* (face to face) of Lord *Visvanātha*. How shall I go? Where to start? How to reach?" The man smiled and said: "Friend, **this** is *Vāraṇasi*; this is the abode of Lord *Viśvanātha*. You do not have to begin anywhere or reach anywhere. YOU ARE HERE!"

In the same way, if 'I' am here, and the Self somewhere else, I will have to learn where and how to start, what *sādhanā* (pursuit for self-unfoldment) to do, and where to reach. But I am myself the beginning and the end. To ask where to begin to realize the Self, is meaningless. Man is always the Self, and nothing else. Dive within. Go to the root within. The Self is within, not outside.

135. THE PASSENGER IN THE CART

The Self is not apart from the body's Activities

A passenger goes in a cart to another village. He falls asleep; but the bullocks move on, at times stand still, at times they are unyoked. The passenger is blissfully unaware of these occurrences; but when he wakes up, finds himself at his destination -- his journey had been completed.

Similarly, the Self is asleep in the body. The waking state is the movement of the bullocks; the *samādhi* (state of absorption) is their standing still -- they are in harness but do not move; so also he is aware but is not attached to actions. The sleeping state is the unyoking of the bullocks; there is complete cessation of activities. Thus work goes on without our consciously attending to it. But because of wrong identification with the body, we think *we* are the doers. Attending to the Self is attending to the work.

[Source: TWRM. 313]

136. THE TRAVELLER ON HORSEBACK

Neither neglect the body nor pamper it.

A traveller on horse-back was returning home from a distant town. He took care of the horse on the way, gave it gram, grass and water, made it rest at intervals so that it would be fit to take its master home safely.

In the same way, so long as we have to travel through life in this body, let us neither neglect the body nor fondle it but care for it properly so that it will serve us in attaining Self-Realization, the goal of life.

[Source: S.S.S.C.]

137. THE POLE THAT WAS FIXED IN THE GROUND

Knowledge about The Truth should be unshakable.

A pole is to be fixed in the ground. A hole is dug, the post placed in it, and the hole is refilled with earth and small stones, and rammed in the well. The post is then shaken to let the filled earth settle in. Then more earth and stones are added, and the process repeated, until no more earth can be added, and the pole is so firmly fixed that it does not yield to any shaking.

Similarly, when a seeker studies the scriptures (*śravana*), it should be accompanied by deep reflection (*manana*) so that the knowledge is firmly fixed, and is doubt-free. Thereafter, no power on earth can create any confusion in the mind. Only then can this unshakable conviction be transformed into experience in *nididhyāsana.*

[Source: B.A. 2]

138. THE SANDALWOOD, SUGARCANE AND THE GOLD

Develop *Prasāda Buddhi.*

When the sandalwood is rubbed again and again against a stone, out of that harsh treatment comes the fragrant sandal paste.

Only when sugarcane is cut and cut again to the lower nodes, does it taste sweeter and sweeter.

Only when the gold is heated in the fire again and again, does it become brighter and brighter.

In the same way, all the trials and tribulations (*hāniḥ*) that occur in our lives are only the Lord's *prasāda* sent to purify us and take us closer to Him. A seeker who is firmly established in Self-knowledge, is able to accept whatever occurs in life with this *prasāda buddhi.* Then alone one has glimpses of the goal i.e. *mokṣa.* All relative transactions become null and void.

[Source: V.D. 12]

139. THE ARMY FACING THE ENEMY IN THE FORT

Self-abidance is surrender to God.

The King's army has laid siege to the enemy's fort. So long as the enemy is in the fort, the men will keep coming out. If the King's army keeps cutting the enemies down as and when they emerge, the fort will fall.

So also, as long as there are *viṣaya vāsanā-s* towards the sense-objects arising in the mind, one should annihilate them through inquiry, then and there, even in the very cradle of their origin. Abiding firmly in the Self (*Ātma-niṣthā*), without giving even the least room for any other thought i.e. thought which is other than the self-thought; is surrendering oneself to God.

[Source: The Path of Sri Ramana-I App. I]

140. THE WORLD REFORMER

To make the world happy, one must become happy oneself.

A man plans to cover the world with leather to avoid the pain caused by walking on stones and thorns, whereas it would be much simpler to wear a pair of shoes on his own feet.

Another tries to tie a cloth over the whole earth to avoid the sun, while, holding an umbrella over his own head in order to shield himself from the sun would be easy and simple.

In the same way, to make the whole world happy, one must find the way of discovering happiness within oneself. This can be done only by finding out about oneself by self-inquiry. When a person realizes himself of being the substratum of the drama of life, he doesn't seek help outside. It comes from within like, Draupadi called *Govinda* and He manifested the way it was required.

The power supporting the world is only one. We are not separate from that *Śakti*.

[Source: LSR. I. 116]

141. LORD KRISHNA AND THE POOR BRAHMIN

Drop the path to reach the Goal.

Once, Lord *Kṛṣṇa* visited his great devotee, a poor Brahmin, whose sole surviving possession was a poor cow which gave him just enough milk for his worship.

Kṛṣṇa blessed the Brahmin by saying: "May that cow die."

Arjuna who was watching this was shocked by his apparent heartlessness towards a devotee. The Lord explained: "Not so, Arjuna. I am indeed helping him in getting rid of his last attachment (*pratibandha*) to the cow."

In *Parā bhakti*, there is no difference between the devotee and the Lord, between the path (the *sādhanā*) and the destination (the *sādhya*). This is *Advaita jñānam* (non-dual knowledge). Only by dropping the *sādhanā* can one go beyond and reach the goal -- the *sādhya*. Otherwise the path can itself become the *pratibandha* (bondage).

[Source: A.A. IX. 35]

142. TWO BIRDS ON A TREE

Two wakers in the same body or Living in Meditation.

Two birds are sitting on an *Aśvattta* tree. They are inseparable companions. One of them is restless; he flits from branch to branch, tasting the different fruits. Some are very tasty, he enjoys; some are sour, he grimaces.

The other bird sits quietly and aloof. He does not participate in the experiences of the fruits. He merely observes and enjoys the antics of his friend alternately enjoying and suffering from the fruits of the tree.

The *Aśvatta* tree is the body. The nature of the body is such that it is constantly in motion, restless . In this body are two birds - the *jīvātmā* (limited being) and *Paramātmā* (Supreme Being). The *jīvātmā* is identified with the body and experiences the various *karma phala* (the fruits); some pleasurable, others not. In the same body is the *Paramātmā* (the second bird), the *kūṭashtha caitanya*, who is not influenced by the good-bad, birth-death, gain-loss relating to the body. These are the two wakers: *jīva* is the one which illumines only the waking world; the *kūṭastha caitanya* is that which illumines the waking world, waking experience, as *also* the *waker*. That which becomes *sukhi* with *sukha*, and *duḥkhī* with *duḥkha* is the *jīva*. That which is unperturbed in spite of the *sukha* or *duḥkha* is the *Paramātmā*. Watch within yourself which is operating at any one moment, in any one experience. That is "living" in meditation.

[Source: M.U. 3.1.1].

143. FINDING A HIDDEN TREASURE

Continued contemplation is the only way to liberation.

A treasure lies buried in the earth. If a person wants to get it, he has no choice except to dig, and to go on digging, whatever the obstacles of hard ground or rock he might encounter, until he finds the treasure. There is no other way.

In the same way, to discover one's own essential nature, other than deeper and deeper contemplation, shedding all thoughts of *saṁsāra*, and dwelling on one's own essential nature (*svātma cintana*), there is no other method.

He digs with the pick-axe of the intellect, removes the rock of gross-body identification, digs the ground of the mind again and again, until he finds the treasure of his own essential nature; and having found it, ...HE HOLDS ON TO IT.

[Source: P.D. IX. 153-4]

144. THE KING WHOSE SON WAS LOST

Ceaseless Meditation will lead to the Truth.

A King's son had gone hunting to the forest, and he got lost. As soon as he heard the news, the King lost not a moment, left no stone unturned and did not rest till he found his lost son.

In the same way, one should strive to know the Truth, casting aside sloth and laziness, and meditate on the Self day and night.

[Source: S.S.S.C]

145. THE MELTED GHEE

Meditation should be unbroken.

The *yajña* is reaching its conclusion. The *purohit-s* around the fire hold long wooden ladles filled with melted ghee and pour it into the *agni* (fire) in one continuous, unbroken stream as the ultimate oblation (*ājya dhārā*) (unbroken flow).

In the same way, the contemplation on the Self should be continuous, uninterrupted by any thought other than of the ONE, and effortless (*sarala cintanam*)

[Source: V.S. 7]

146. THE CHURNING OF THE *YAJNA* FIRE

Intense contemplation of *Māhāvākya-s* (Supreme Truth) produces the fire of Self-Knowledge.

The fire for the *yajña* is to be started. The two-piece wooden *araṇi* is taken. The peg of the upper *araṇi* is fixed in the hollow of the lower *araṇi* and churned fast. The friction generates sparks of fire. A piece of fibre is placed at this point so as to catch the fire from the sparks, and the burning piece of fibre is transferred to the *yajña kuṇḍa* to start the *agni.*

In the same way, the mind is the lower *araṇi.* In this is fixed the upper *araṇi* of Vedānta mahāvākya-s or the praṇava (OṀ Sound). Through the processes of *śravaṇam, mananam* and *nididhyāsanam,* the meaning of these vākya-s is analyzed again and again. By this process of churning *(nirmathanam),* the fire of knowledge is produced. This *jñāna* is such that it burns up the bondage of *saṁsāra,* just as the *yajña* fire burns up everthing that is offered to it as oblation.

[Source: Kai.U. II]

147. THE FATHER AND HIS NEW-BORN SON

Non-dual meditation.

A father looks at his new-born son. He sees himself in his son; and therefore gives him all that he would have given himself. Love for the son is natural because the son is not other than the father.

Similarly, when the Lord is seen as separate from oneself *(bheda bhrama)*, meditation requires effort. But when the *bhāvanā* is *abheda*, that the Lord and I are one, this contemplation of non-dual existence is Supreme. Spontaneous, effortless love manifests naturally as the total identity between the beloved Lord and the *jīva* (limited being).

[Source: V.S. 8]

148. THE MAN WHO WANTED TO KNOW WHAT HE WAS

Silence is the Real State.

A man wants to know what he is. He is told: "Look around you. There are so many animals and objects. Are you a cow?" "No, I am not." "Fine. You are not a cow nor a horse nor a tree nor a duck, nor this nor that ..."

The man protests: "But you have not told me what I am." The reply comes: "I did not say you are not a man. You must find that out yourself!"

In the same way, the scriptures tell us: "You are not the body nor the mind nor the intellect nor the ego, not this, nor this *(neti neti iti),* nor anything that you can think of." Thus having eloquently negated everything, they are silent.
This silence denotes the Real State. It denotes that the questioner himself is the Self that is being sought. When the source of the I thought is reached, it vanishes. What remains over is the Self - the silence.

[Source: TWRM.620]

149. THE SAGE AND THE HUNTER

The "Fourth State"

In a forest, a great *Muni* sat in a lotus posture with his eyes open, in deep trance. A hunter hit a deer with his arrow, but the deer escaped, ran in front of the sage, and hid in a nearby bush. The hunter came in pursuit of the deer and asked the sage: "Where did the deer go?" The sage replied: "My friend, I don't know." In disbelief, the hunter asked: "*Svāmi* (master), it ran right in front of you, and your eyes are open. How did you not see?!"

In the waking, dream and deep sleep states, the ego operates. But when one is submerged in the Self, one is said to be in the "fourth" *(Turiya)* state, where the ego is no more operative. The mind is totally destroyed *(mano nāśa)*. There is no merging *(laya)* and emerging which is only a stage of *sadhana* (pursuit of the self). One is not conscious of what is happening around. The 'I' becomes one's very nature *(svarūpa)*. It does not matter whether the eyes are open or closed.

150. THE MAN WHO WOKE UP FROM SLEEP

One "Becomes" what one meditates upon

A man was asleep. He dreamt. In the dream, he had many experiences -- He suffered and he enjoyed.

Then he woke up. He rubbed his eyes, "Ah, all that was only a dream. Now I have woken up. This is the real Me!," he thought with relief.

Thus the dreamer had "become" the waker. But he had not really "become" someone new. Earlier in the dream state, he had temporarily disowned his waker-hood. On "becoming" the waker, he was only reclaiming his real wakerhood.

In the same way, a seeker, by long and sustained *nididhyāsana* (contemplation) on the *nirguṇa Brahman* (without attributes) which is *viśokam* (without grief), *anantam* (infinite), etc. "becomes" what he has meditated upon -- the *Brahma Tattva* itself. *"Brahmavit Brahmaiva bhavati* (Knower of *Brahma* becomes *Brahma*)." In owning the *jīva-hood* (limited being), he had temporarily disowned *Brahman-hood* (universal self). Now, he reclaims that ownership.

151. THE CATERPILLAR AND THE BUTTERFLY

As your *Bhāvanā* (nature of thought), so you become.

From the moment, it hatches out of the egg, the caterpillar has only one object -- to metamorphose into a butterfly. This is the only thought governing its existence even while it is lying dormant inside the chrysalis. Till one day, at one moment, it emerges as a butterfly and realizes the self-image it has been nursing all along.

In the same way, when the *bhāvanā abhyāsa* (the realization of nature of thought) of *"aham Brahmāsmi* (I am the *Brahman*)" is done again and again, suddenly it "happens" -- *Bhramatakitavat.* Thereafter, there is no more trying to "become"; ONE "is".

[Source: B.A. 19]

152. THE MAN WHO ATTEMPTS TO SLEEP

Meditation-less Meditaton

A person tosses in bed, counts sheep, and tries all methods to make himself go to sleep. At last sleep overtakes him. Once he has slept, all "attempts to sleep" cease. To the sleeper, there is no more anxiety to sleep, for he is already asleep.

In the same way, once you have realized that you are indeed the Self, there is no more need to meditate on the nature of the Self.

TO GIVE UP MEDITATION THROUGH MEDITATION
IS THE HIGHEST MEDITATION.

There is no greater meditation than meditation-less meditation. It is infinite fulfilment. It is the end of the way, the last leap into the goal. Here yoga ends. Self as Self revels in the Self.

[Source: Ast.G. XV. 20]

153. THE REBELLIOUS CHILD AND THE *MAHÀTMA*

Abheda Dṛṣṭi - The Goal of Upāsanā

A child once refused to do his daily *pūja* (worship) in a spirit of rebellion. A *mahātmā* (a great soul) who was watching the scene took the child to the terrace and pointing to the street below, asked, "What do you see from here?"

The child replied: "I see lots of people, buses, cycles, cars, children, a balloon-man ... And you, uncle, what do you see?"

The *Mahātmā* replied: "I see only *Bhagavān Kṛṣṇa* (Lord Krishna) everywhere."

This *abheda dṛṣṭi* is the purpose and goal of *upāsanā*.

Jagata Īśadhi yuktasevanam
Aṣṭamūrtibhṛt devapūjanam

[U.S. 5]

When this *anvaya abhyāsa* of seeing the *Paramātmā* as permeating all forms is done, the mortal becomes immortal; one attains *Brahmattva*, even here.

[Source: V.D. 21]

154. GANGA MEETING THE OCEAN

There is No Difference between 'I' and 'That'

The river *Gaṅgā* meets the ocean *(sāgara)*, the place where 'she' meets 'him' is called *Gaṅgā-sāgara*. *Gaṅgā* is feminine gender, *sāgara* is masculine gender, but *Gaṅgā sāgara* is neither. The two are glorified by one word. Thereafter, it is not possible to say which is *gaṅgā* water and which is ocean water. It is just one expanse of water, neuter, beyond the two genders.

In the same way, when the devotee meets the Lord, there is no difference - The Consciousness expressing as devotee, saluting the Lord, and the Lord expressing His own Glory are one and the same. When *dvaita* (duality) disappears, knowledge dawns.

[Source A.A. II. 54]

155. THE FARMER'S DILEMMA ABOUT HIS HEN

Jīva-Jagat-Īśvara (Individual Being, World & The Lord) constitute one entity.

A farmer owned a hen which served him well by laying eggs. A feast-day came, and it was suggested that the hen be killed for dinner. Now, the farmer was in a dilemma. He wanted the hen for laying eggs; he also wanted to cook her for dinner. If only he could cut her in two, use one part for laying eggs, and the other for dinner!

He knew that this was impossible. He had to forego one of the purposes and be content with the other: either keep the whole hen for eggs or eat the whole hen for dinner.

In the same way, the *jīva-jagat-Īśvara* are one indivisible whole: any one implies the other two. The first two are the effects for which the third is the cause, which permeates and sustains the other two (the effect).

Therefore, for inquiry, all three must be treated as a whole, as one three-fold entity, either to be rejected as unreal or to be treated as real. There is no middle course of treating one component as real and the others as unreal.

156. MEETING THE SAME PERSON AT DIFFERENT TIMES

Identity between the *Jīvātmā* (Individual Soul) and Paramātmā (Supreme Soul).

I met a person yesterday evening. I met him in the market; he was wearing a *dhoti* and *kurta.* I met him again this morning at the bus-stop. He was wearing pant and shirt. Although I met him at different locations, at different times and in different attires, I could recognize him as one and the same person. The differences were of no consequence.

In the same way, the qualities of *tat (the Brahman),* and *tvam (the jīva)* may appear completely different e.g. inside-outside (the body), little knowledge-omniscience, little power-infinite power etc.. But they should be ignored as incidental. The substratum of both is only pure consciousness *(śuddha caitanya).*

[Source: D.M.S., M.U. III. 13-15]

157. THE LOST TENTH MAN

Discovery of the Self as the Nearest of the Near.

Ten foolish men crossed a river. On reaching the other bank, each counted the others to check if all had reached safe, and each one found one man missing. So all of them grieved for the "lost" tenth man. A wise man passing by understood their problem and pointed out to each man: "O friend, the tenth man is not lost; the tenth man is you yourself."

Once each man understood that the nine were "other than himself," and that he himself was the tenth man, there was rejoicing; no more *āyāsa* (effort) in finding the tenth man. It was a gain of what had already been gained.

In the same way, we imagine the nine *upādhi-s* (modifications) of *viṣaya* (objects), *deha* (body), *indriya* (senses), *prāṇa* (breaths), *mana* (mind), *buddhi* (intellect), *ahaṁkāra* (i-ness), and *ajñānam* (ignorance) to be ourselves, and thus miss the real I. If we can separate these *upādhi-s* (modifications) as mere objects of cognition, then we discover that our own essential nature is *Brahma svarūpa.* It is present in all places, at all times, in every situation, closest to one, nearest of the near, one's own *(svasya Brahma)* (Self is *Brahma*).

This is *Brahma Vijñānam* (Knowledge of the Self).

[Source: V.D. 75-83. P.D. VII.]

158. THE *GURU* SITTING ON THE BANK OF THE *GANGA*

Seeing the Divine Presence Every Moment.

Once a *Guru* was sitting on the river bank. His hand was idly playing with the sand. His disciple stood by watching. The *Guru* turned and asked: "What do you see?" The disciple replied: "I see sand in your hand."

The *Guru* replied: "When you see *Paramātmā* (Supreme Being) in the sand, then you are somewhere near the Truth."

In the same way, when the mind is soaked with the thought of the Divine presence everywhere, in everything, every moment, then out of long habit, the mind becomes one with the theme called the Truth.

[Source: A.A. IX. 9]

159. THE *MAHATMA* GOING FOR *BHIKSHA*

Receiving Divine message in every sound.

A great *Mahātmā* (great soul) once went to a house for *bhikṣā* (alms). Instead of *bhikṣā*, he received an outpour of abuses from the man of a house. The *Mahātmā* stood still till the *"Sahasranama archana (thousand names recital)"* was over. Saying, "You are shameless," the man finally turned away in disgust.

A strong disciple, unable to tolerate this insult to his *Guru* said: "Please allow me to give back what he gave and settle accounts." The Master said: "I agree, one must give back if one has received. But I have 'received' nothing."

In the same way, let us take all harsh words that we receive as spiritual *sādhanā*. Let us cultivate that faculty (the third ear) by which every sound only reminds us of His Presence. *Bhagavān Kṛṣṇa* said: "Not only am I the *Oṁkāra* in the *Veda-s*; but in the space - the sound I am, every sound." [B.G. VII-8]
If this line of thinking is cultivated, nothing in the world will disturb us.

Bhadraṁ karṇebhiḥ śṛṇuyāma devāḥ

160. THE SUN AND THE DARKNESS

The Self is revealed in the contact between SUBJECT and OBJECT.

The sun, out of great compassion went to lift the darkness with his one thousand arms. When he embraced the darkness, both the darkness and light, disappeared. There was no one whom he could help. There was none, other than himself.

In the same way, subject and object exist simultaneously in I, the Pure Consciousness. When the subject and object come in contact, the essential Self is revealed. The *bheda* (difference) between the seer (the *viṣayī,* follower of the objects) and the seen (the *viṣaya,* objects) disappears. "Becoming" ends, only "Being" remains.

[Source: A.A. IX. 24]

161. THE FIG FRUIT

The Source is a point without dimensions.

On the bidding of his father, ***Śvetaketu*** took the fruit of the banyan (fig) tree and broke it open. Inside, he saw many tiny seeds like grains. His father bade him to open one of the grains and asked: "What do you see?" "Nothing," replied the boy. On the subtleness of this seed which one cannot perceive, stands the whole big banyan tree, with its trunk, branches, leaves, fruits etc.

In the same way, the gross universe which is possessed of names and forms is born from Existence which is very subtle. The source is a point without dimensions. It expands as the cosmos on one hand, and as Infinite Bliss on the other. From this point starts a *vāsanā* which multiplies as the experiencer (I), the experience and the world of experience. This subtle point, the essence, is the Truth. It is the Self. You are that.

[Sources: C.U. VI. 12. 1 to 3, TWRM. 616, B.A.22-24]

162. THE TWO STONE DOGS

The Self manifests where the world is not.

A man wanted to see the King's palace. As he approached, he saw two dogs on either side of the palace gateway, and so hesitated to go near.

Seeing his predicament, a wise man passing by, took him by the hand and said: "Come with me friend, there is nothing to fear."

When the man got close enough to see clearly, he discovered that there were no dogs, only stone carving of dogs!

In the same way, if you see the world, the Self will not be visible; if you see the Self, the world will not be visible. If you see the stone, it does not mean the dogs ran away. The world will continue to be; but your *dṛṣṭi* (vision) will be on the Self alone.

[Source: LSR. II. 6]

163. THE SUN THAT ENTERED THE WATER

The One Alone appears as many.

The sun is a bright orb in the sky. It is reflected in the lake below. Suddenly, a breeze blows and causes ripples on the lake's surface. The reflection breaks and now appears as many suns.

In the same way, the One and only *Parabrahma Paramātmā* (total cosmic Self) enters the various bodies and appears as many.

[Source: D.M.S., M.U. 3.31]

164. THE TWO FLUTES

There is no differentiation in *Paramātma tattva* (Essence of Supreme Self), only in its expression.

Two students are practising on the flute. The two flutes look alike. The air that is blown through the two flutes is also the same. But from one flute, the student produces only noise; from the other, the second student creates melodious music. Although there is no difference in the flutes or in the air blown through them, there is a difference in the expression that emerged.

In the same way, the Self is present in every object *(sarva gatam).* The objects are many, but the Self does not undergo any differentiation. There is no sense of other-ness, of *bheda,* of knower-known-knowledge. The "I-Am-ness" is constant.

165. THE REFLECTED FACE

One-ness is the Reality.

One knows one has a face; that face is oneself. Then one wants to see one's own face. So a duality is created with the help of a mirror. I (the knower, the original face) "enters" the mirror, and I (the known) "comes out" as the reflection. Thus the knower-known, subject-object dichotomy is just a game. The one-ness of the source is never denied.

In every experience, this one-ness is sought, where there is only experiencing and no experiencer or experienced. **Living in this experience is meditation.** This one-ness is the Reality.

[Source: A.A. IV. 2]

166. THE RAINDROPS

Manifestation is the Truth Alone.

A boy sits at the window watching the raindrops fall. He counts them as they fall: one, two, three .... He looks down to see where they have fallen. He cannot see the drops, but only a puddle where the drops fell. Where have the raindrops gone? He cannot count them individually anymore in the puddle. It is only water now.

Similarly, the world is nothing but the manifestation (the raindrops) of that One Truth (water). Just as the manifestation of raindrops shows that there is nothing other than water, so in the manifestation of the world, there is nothing other than the Truth.

[Source: A.A.9]

167. THE ROCK CARVING

The same consciousness expresses as many-ness.

Out of one huge rock are carved the temple, the presiding deity, the followers of the deity etc..

In the same way, the *śuddha caitanya* (pure consciousness) is expressed as the multiplicity - of the Divine, the devotee and the devotion. There is no difference between the *Paramātmā* (Supreme Self) and his devotees.

[Source: A.A. IX 42]

168. THE MOON AND THE MOONLIGHT

***Paramātmā* (Supreme Self) reveals Himself in every name and form.**

It is a full-moon day. The moon is covered by moonlight. But this does not mean that the moon is "hidden" by the moonlight or that we should take a lamp to see the moon. The moon and the moonlight are not two.

In the same way, every name and form has the potentiality to remind us of the Divine Essence. There is infinite choice for the *Paramātmā* to reveal Himself. With this vision, there is nothing to dislike.

[Source: A.A. II 56]

169. THE GOLD AND ORNAMENTS FOR THE KING'S CORONATION

No difference or differentiation in Pure Consciousness.

Different ornaments were made for a king and his queen for their coronation: *nāga* (masculine) for the upper arm, a *mundī* (feminine) ring for the finger, and *kaṅkaṇa* (neuter gender) for the wrist.

Although the ornaments were referred to differently according to their gender, essentially, they were the same gold. Gold includes all the three genders.

Similarly, out of this Supreme I or Pure Consciousness is the experiencer (masculine or feminine), experience (no gender) and the experienced (neuter gender). The Pure Consciousness has no difference or differentiation.

[Source: A.A. IX. 12]

170. THE DISCIPLE WHO WANTED THE LORD'S *DARSHAN*

The Supreme Self cannot be concealed.

A disciple approached a *Mahātmā* (great soul) and requested: "Please give me the *darśana* (vision) of *Bhagavān* (Lord)."

He waited, and repeated his request twice, thrice ...

The Maharaj in exasperation shook his stick at him and said: "The Lord is all around you, in the sun and the moon, in all things and beings; everything is *Paramātmā* (Supreme Self) alone. And yet you keep saying, you cannot see the Lord!"

The glorious expression of the Universal Consciousness cannot conceal the Supreme in anyway. The clouds cannot hide the sun; even they exist because of the sun.
Even the statement, "I cannot see God," is because of His Presence. He does not hide Himself. One has only to develop the subtlety of vision to see His Presence, all the time, everywhere.
"Eṣu sarveṣu bhūteṣu gūḍhātmā na prakāśate."

171. THE SWEETNESS IN THE SWEET MEATS

Seeing the Self as Self.

At the feast, many kinds of sweets with various ingredients have been prepared, in various sizes and shapes and colours. In spite of this variety in their appearance, they all taste sweet. There is nc difference in their sweetness, because there is sugar in all of them and sweetness is the nature of sugar.

In the same way, all experiences are enlivened by the illumination which is the nature of the Self. Without the Self, no experience can be experienced, just as without sugar, no food can taste sweet.

[Source: D.D.V]

172. THE INDEFATIGABLE FARMER

Self-Realization requires long patient practice.

A farmer inherited a piece of land. He tilled the land, sowed good seeds, watered and watched over the crop. The land did not yield much the first year. But he did not give up. He tried again the next year, the next and the next, with the same care and love, and ever-increasing zeal and faith; till at last his labours were rewarded with a rich harvest.

In the same way, the realization of *Brahman* does not come in a day. It requires long and sustained effort. One should persevere if there is lack of success in the early stages. One should continue the *abhyāsa* (practice) with ever-renewed vigour.

"Nitya abhyāsāt ṛte prāptiḥ na bhavet saccidātmanaḥ."

173. THE *AKASHA* (SPACE) IN THE WELL

Realization is not discovering something New.

A well is being dug. A huge pit is "created." The *ākāśa* (space in the well was not "created" by the digger; only the earth filling the space was removed. The *ākāśa* was there earlier, it is there now.

Similarly, it is incorrect to speak of "realization". There is nothing to "realize". The "real" is always as it is. Thus far, we have "realized" only the un-reals, i.e. taken as real all that is unreal, namely the age-long *saṁskāra-s* (tendencies) inside us. When all that is thrown out, the Self *(ākāśa)* alone shines. All that is required to attain *jnāna* (knowledge) is a change of attitude. Nothing is created anew, nothing is achieved that one did not already have before.

[Source: D.D.V.]

174. THE SANDALWOOD

Divinity is revealed when *vāsanā-s* are removed.

The sandalwood has captivating fragrance. When it is left in water for a long time, it emits a bad smell. When taken out and rubbed against a stone, the bad-smelling surface is removed, and the divine fragrance emerges again.

Similarly, although we are the *Ātman* (soul); because of our identification with the body, all bad behaviour comes out. And with spiritual practice, all the bad odour of the *vāsanā-s* (tendencies) get removed, the mind gets purified, and the fragrance of one's own essential nature, the Supreme Self is revealed.
Divinity does not have to be "given" from somewhere else. It is always with us.

[Source: V.C. 274]

175. THE MAN WHO BLEW OUT THE LIGHT IN THE ROOM

Reality is revealed in absence.

A man entered a room at dusk and lit a candle. The whole room was filled with light.

After some time, he blew out the candle. The room was now in darkness. When he put out the light, did he also disappear?

He is the one who established the presence of the light, and he is the one who established the absence of the light.

In the same way, that Presence which is present in the presence of the waker of the waking state, and the dreamer of the dream-state, and which is also present in the absence of both in the deep sleep state, is the Reality.
Total absence is silence.
When absence is contemplated upon, one hears the "sound of silence," the sound that is beyond relative sound and relative silence, beyond knowledge and the bondage of knowledge.

[Source: A.A. IV 28-29]

176. THE FRUIT AND CONTENTMENT

When Truth is revealed, all words lose meaning.

The clouds disappear after they pour down rain. When the road reaches the portico of the house, it ends. It does not go anywhere else.

The fruit destroys itself in revealing the juice, and the juice disappears in revealing contentment.

In the same way, the words - *Sat* (Truth), *Cit* (consciousness), and *Ānanda* (bliss), *Ātmā* (soul) disappear after revealing the essential nature of the Truth, and after removing the earlier delusion of *asat* (untruth), *acit* (non-conscious) and *duḥkham* (pain).

[Source: A.A. V]

177. THE FLOWER'S SELF-ANNIHILATION TO REACH FULFILMENT

The words *Sat, Cit, Ananda* disappear when Truth is revealed.

The flower of the mango tree dries up and destroys itself to reveal the fruit, the fruit destroys itself to reveal the juice, and the juice destroys itself to reveal total contentment.

In the same way, the words *sat, cit and ananda* destroy themselves in removing the earlier delusion of *asat, acit and duḥkham.* Thereafter there is only total fulfilment. This contentment does not "die" to yield something else. It is itself the end of the road, the ultimate destination, a state of no loss-no gain, a state of "stateless-ness." "That on gaining which, he feels there is no greater gain and that in which he abides...." [B.G. VI 23]

[Source: A.A. v. 22]

178. THE WAX DOLLS

Obliteration of 'I vs. This' difference.

A doll-maker found no market for his wax-dolls. So he melted them all together. Now the space between the dolls is obliterated.

In the same way, in the Supreme Truth, all separate-ness and sense of other-ness is gone. This is the *Viśvarūpa darśana*, where everything is included in the Lord. All objectivity is negated. This is the state of void, total absence. There is no *aham-idam bheda* (difference of 'I' and 'not I')

[Source: B.A. 22-24]

179. THE LUMP OF EARTH AND OF GOLD

The product is not different from the material cause

or

Knowing that by which all else become known.

By knowing a lump of earth, all things made of earth are known. All modifications are only in the name and the form.

So also by knowing a lump of gold, all things made of gold become known. Gold is the reality. All modifications are only in the name, for which different words are used.

Similarly, everything is nothing but the one *Paramātma Tattva.* When in the world of names and forms, the *Pūrṇa Tattva* (complete essence) is discovered, then one comes to understand that one's own essential nature is also the same *Pūrṇa Paramātma Rūpam.*

[Source: V.D. 35, C.U. VI.]

180. *BRAHMAJI'S* PRIDE AS BEING THE OLDEST

Longevity - not synonymous with Realization.

Once *Brahmāji* boasted to *Viṣṇu* that he was the greatest because he was the longest lived. *Viṣṇu* said that it was not so, as there were several others older than *Brahmā.* To prove his point, he took *Brahmā* to *Romāsa Muni* (one covered with hair) and asked him how old he was and how long he expected to live. That *Muni* said that one hair on his body dropped when one *Brahma* died, a *Brahma's* life being one hundred years, each *Brahma* day being the equivalent of one *yuga.* When all the hairs on his body dropped, he would die.

Then *Viṣṇu* took *Brahmā* to *Aṣṭāvakra Ṛṣi,* and asked him the same question. That sage replied that when one *Romāsa Muni's* hair will fall, one of his distortion would disappear. When all his eight distortions disappear, he would die. *Brahmāji* felt crestfallen.

Similarly, one may do various penance like breath control etc. to prolong one's life, but one does not become a *jñāni* (knowledgable) by living long. A realized person has no love for his body. For him who is the embodiment of bliss, the body is only a disease and a burden. He regards his body in the same way as a coolie regards his load. He looks forward to pulling down the load at the destination.

181. THE ACTOR

Seeing the Self is abiding in the Self.

An actor puts on different costumes for different roles. When he casts off all these costumes, what remains is the person himself, as he is a person without the acts.

In the same way, when through proper *vicāra* (inquiry), one rejects all that is not-self (all the costumes and the role playing), one has the vision of one's own Self without superimposing the conditioning roles. This is 'Self-realization'.
It is the same as God-realization (*Īśa darśanam*).
Because the Lord is none other than the Self (*svātmarūpataḥ*)

[Source: V.S. 25]

182. THE DUMB PERSON

The State of Supreme Bliss.

A dumb person does have various experiences, but he cannot speak about them.

A mirror reflects every object that comes before it, but retains no image.

In the same way, a mind that has conquered habitual thinking, becomes emptied of thoughts. It does not react; the tongue does not speak. Such a divine mind is a state of the Divine Presence. This state of Supreme Bliss is liberation.

Jite tasmin vṛtti śūnyaṁ
manaḥ tiṣṭhati mūkavat

[Source: P.D. IV. 63]

183. THE MAN WHO THOUGHT HE WAS VERY WISE

Bliss of *Brahman* must be 'experienced' to attain the state of fulfilment.

An announcement was once made that a reward would be given to one who knew the four *Veda-s.* A person promptly put in his claim for the prize. "Do you know the four *Veda-s*?," he was asked. "Sure I do, I know that there are four *Veda-s*: *Ṛg, Yajur* etc. etc.. So, give me the award!"

In the same way, just by sitting quiet (in *tuṣṭhi sthiti*), one does not automatically get the bliss of *Brahman.* The quietness that one experiences just before dropping off to sleep or just on waking up, is only a fleeting fore-flash of *Brahmānanda.* It is not the real thing; it will not lead to fulfilment. Knowing about *Brahman* does not mean one has attained *Brahmānanda,* which is very subtle and can be reached only by proper study of the scriptures and the guidance of the *Guru.*

[Source: P.D. XI. 77-81]

184. THE DOCTOR'S PRESCRIPTION

Activity destroys one's inherent happiness.

A doctor advised his patient to take a prescribed medicine. He specified only one condition that the patient should not think of a monkey when he takes the medicine.

Will the patient ever be able to take the medicine? Whenever he tries to do so, he will only think of the monkey.

In the same way, to advise the seeker "to do" this or that, to realize the Self is not a help. Activity is creation, the destruction of one's inherent happiness.
When one "tries" to give up thoughts, the person gets frustrated by the very attempt. One can attain only that, which is not already attained. In realizing one's true nature, there is nothing to be attained. ONE'S VERY BEING IS THAT.

[Source: TWRM. 601]

185. POT WITH WATER

Moving from *Bhāva* to *Anubhava* for the bliss of Self.

A person was thirsty and was looking for cold water. He saw a big pot but did not know if it contained water and if so, how much. So he placed his hands on the pot's belly and, by the feel of the coolness, he could *infer* that there was water more than half the pot.

In the same way, by long and continuous *samādhi abhyāsa* (practice of meditation), one develops the subtlety of vision by which the bliss of the Self can be "inferred". Gradually, with further practice, the 'I-am-ness' is dissolved. The knower-known difference disappears. Forgetfulness of the individuality is the discovery of the Reality. One moves from *nijānanda bhāva* (self-knowledge attitude) to *nijānanda anubhava* (bliss-experience) itself.

[Source: P.D. XI.98]

186. THE KING WHO IS HAPPY

True Happiness is obtained by growing out of desires.

A wise and young king is full of happiness: He has health, wealth, youth, is well-endowed and all-powerful. He lacks nothing. Even so, his happiness is only one hundredth of the happiness of *Brahmā*; *Brahmā's* happiness is only one-hundredth of that of the *Gandharva-s* and so on and on, up the ladder of the happiness of the *pitṛ-s*, the *deva-s, Indra, Bṛhaspati* etc.. And all the happiness of all these levels put together is but a fraction of the bliss of *Brahman!*

True happiness lies not in possessing things but in growing out of the desire for things.
This bliss (unalloyed and complete) of *Brahman* is realized by *Brahmniṣṭhā* who is free from cravings. He experiences the joy that exceeds the sum of relative happiness of all levels.

[Source: T.U. II. 8, V.D. 77]

187. THE TIGER WHO TASTED HUMAN BLOOD

**The seeker of the bliss of Self
loses taste for worldly themes.**

Once a tiger has tasted human blood, therafter it loses all taste for animal blood.

In the same way, once the priority in our life changes, when knowing one's own essential nature becomes our prime and intense concern, there will be no more taste for worldly themes and thoughts. One starts enjoying solitude; one starts listening to silence *(Rahasi sthitaḥ).*
The purpose of all *kriya* (action), all discussion, is only to enter this abode of peace.

[Source: V.D. 12]

188. THE *SHAKUNI* BIRD

Going back to the source.

A *Śakuni* bird was secured to a tree by a long string tied to its leg. He constantly tried to fly out in all directions hither and thither, but could go only as far as the length of the string allowed him.

After some time, he got totally exhausted and not finding any place to rest his tired wings, came back to the branch to which he was tied; the source. Now he found rest.

In the same manner, the mind, which is a conditioning of the *jīva*, is constantly moving in the dream and waking states; from person to person, place to place, time to time, experience to experience. Ultimately, when all the *karma-s* (actions) which are responsible for the positive and negative experiences are exhausted, he goes back to his own source. Now, he has only one desire - to rest in *Brahmānanda* (supreme bliss).

[Source: P.D. XI. 49]

189. THE OLD LADY AND THE LOST NEEDLE

Supreme bliss is closest to us.

An old lady was searching for something under the street light. A young man observing this enquired what she was looking for.

"For a needle," came the reply, as she continued her search. The young man also started searching. Presently he asked: "When exactly did it fall, amma?" Promptly came the response: "Oh, I dropped it in my house. There is no light in the house. There is light here. So I am searching here as I cannot search in darkness!"

In the same way, we search for bliss by running after worldly objects; while all the time, bliss is in our own bosom as our own essential nature.

"Ahaṁ eva paraṁ Brahma"
(I alone am the Supreme Self)

[Source: B.A. 1]

190. THE POOR LITTLE MAID

Bliss lies in oneself.

A guest at a friend's house woke up to hear a young girl's dear voice singing a beautiful song about a crimson *sāri* - How pretty it was, how fine its embroidery, how beautiful its border, *pallu* etc..

Moved by the happy song, he went to see who was singing it. It was the poor little maid-servant of the house who was herself in poor rags, but none-the-less merry. Taking pity on her, he gifted her a pretty *sāri*. Her joy knew no bounds. Wearing it later, she whirled and danced with her friends as if she owned the earth. The following morning, when she came to work, she was back in her old clothes, just as merry as ever, with no trace of regret or depression.

Happiness lies not in external objects but in oneself (*yena tyaktena*). Man should enjoy whatever is bestowed on him by God with the firm conviction that it is for one's good. To be contented with one's slot in life, is to be in bliss.

[Source: S.U., S.S.S.C.]

191. THE FORGOTTEN KEY

The key to bliss is with us alone.

One dark cold night, a king stood outside his own palace gate and waited, forgetting that the key to the palace was in his own pocket. All he had to do was to take it, unlock the gate, and walk into the warmth and joy of his home.

In the same way, the scriptures tell us to end our life's sorrows by taking the key that is always with us, and open the doors to our own palace, our own kingdom within. Bliss is *svarūpa*. Let us open the gate to this temple of Bliss, with the key of *Ātma Kṛpā*.

192. THE HAILSTONE THAT FELL INTO THE OCEAN

The experience of infinitude cannot be described.

There is a hailstorm. A hailstone falls on the vast expanse of the ocean. It may sink a few yards below the surface; thereafter, there is no more going or coming. It becomes the ocean itself.

Similarly, the mind which is in deep meditation can go only thus far ... Thereafter, it is not possible to express in words the experience of the infinitude, nor can the mind even think about it. All that can be said is that it is *ānanda*. It is complete sense of fulfilment. It is a joy, untouched by the fear of loss.
When the mind meditates on *Brahman*, it becomes *Brahman*. There is no 'this', nor 'that', only "is-ness".

[Source: V.C. 483-5]

193. THE KING IN DISGUISE

Tragedies of the body do not touch the man of wisdom.

A king went one day to the market place disguised as a beggar. He sat down along with other beggars and begged. It was only a sport for him. He knew he was the royal lord of his kingdom. The royal robes beneath the rags assured him of that.

Similar is the case with the *jīvan mukta*, who has experienced the bliss of infinitude in himself. He may move about in the physical body and experience all the vicissitudes of life, but he takes them all as sport. He is no longer affected by them nor does he get involved in them.

[Source: V.C. 347]

194. THE LEAF-PLATES

A *Jnānī's* (Knower-Enlightened) disregard for the body.

At a marriage feast, food is served on beautifully stitched leaf-plates. However beautiful they may be, they are thrown away once the meal is over, with no regrets.

In the same way, after attaining the Supreme Knowledge, one only waits eagerly for the time when the body can be thrown away. He has no more regard for the body nor regret in dropping it.

[Source: L.S.R. 123]

195. THE HUNTER WHO SHOT AN ARROW AT A TIGER

***Prārabdha* (Destiny) of the body has to run its course.**

A hunter, thinking that there was a tiger among the bushes, aimed his arrow at it and shot it. As the arrow left the bow and was winging its way to the target, he realized that it was a cow. But that knowledge could neither stop the arrow in its flight, nor could it change the arrow's course. The arrow, once shot, has to reach its target.

In the same way, the body is the arrow that has already been shot from the bow of past thoughts, desires and actions. Propelled by the force of these thoughts and desires, the body has perforce to go through the convulsions of sufferings and enjoyments. Nothing can stop or change this course. A realized man knows this and accepts it, and is not involved in the experiences of the body. He does not attribute it to the Self.

[Source: V.C. 452-3]

196. THE *RISHI* AND THE TWIN CALVES

Saṅkalpa-less Buddhi.

A devotee gifted a cow to a *ṛṣi* (a sage). The cow yielded twin calves. The *ṛṣi* tied the calves together with a long rope, thinking he could keep a better watch on them.

A camel came along and lifted the calves by the rope which was binding them. Hearing the calves cry, the *ṛṣi* ran out and saw them dangling helplessly in the air.

"Ah," he lamented, "O desire, I now know your birth-place. You are born out of *saṅkalpa.* If I had not made a *saṅkalpa* that, 'If I had a cow, I will have plenty of milk,' I would not be experiencing this anguish now."

In the same way, *saṅkalpa* creates bondage. The man of wisdom stays in the world, enjoys every moment, then forgets about it. He entertains no *saṅkalpa*, no expectation of repeating the experience. This is called *prasāda buddhi.* Desire-less, *saṅkalpa-less buddhi* aids liberation.

[Source: P.D. VII 170]

197. THE ROASTED SEED

Desires do not create dependence in a man of wisdom.

There were two farmers. One sowed good seed, and they germinated and grew up into new plants which produced more seeds and so on.

The other farmer sowed roasted seeds. None germinated. But the same seeds when ground, made good food.

In the same way, the man of ignorance and the man of wisdom; both have desires. The former develops dependence on their fulfilment as they go on multiplying. The desires in the man of wisdom are like roasted seeds. They do not generate more desires which would drive him into a frenzy of worldly activities, because he has true knowledge about the illusory nature of the world. The ignorant man's action is born out of compulsion to fulfill desire; the wise man's action is born out of joy.

[Source: P.D. VII 163-4]

198. THE TWO KINGS

The wise man is not deluded by worldly enjoyment.

There were two kings. One lost his kingdom in a war and was taken captive. When he was released from bondage and given a small village, he was quite happy. Having suffered the pangs of limited existence in prison, he was happy just to be free.

The other king who was totally free, yet was not satisfied even with his whole kingdom, having experienced the unlimited existence of freedom.

In the same way, a man of discrimination who has discovered the limitations of worldly enjoyments will no longer hanker after them. He will be perfectly contented with the fulfilment of minimum needs.

[Source: P.D. VII 150]

199. THE ROTATING TOP

The Realized Sage is ever Active.

A fast rotating gyroscope is apparently still. Its speed cannot be followed by the eye, and therefore it appears to be still. Yet it is rotating very fast.

So is the apparent inaction of the sage. People mistake it to be inertia. It is not so. His non-action is eternal and intense activity. "By his non-action, the sage governs all."

[Source: TWRM. 599]

200. THE RED BERRIES

Doershiр is superimposed on the man of wisdom.

Two men walking in the country-side, see what seems to be a house on fire. They go towards the bright glow. But when they come near the house, they see no fire, but only big bushes around the house, laden with bright red berries. They had only imagined that the red glow was fire. The fire was only a superimposition which could not burn either the house or the plants.

Similarly, on the man of wisdom, others superimpose doership, but the duties and actions that he performs, do not touch him. He does not come under the influence of relative existence. He observes the modifications without a feeling of participation.

[Source: P.D. VII. 258-9]

201. THE RUBBER BALL

The *Jīvan mukta's* (Liberation while living) devotion is involuntary and continuous.

A rubber ball placed on a table rolls off the edge, drops down, bounces up, again comes down, and so on on its own, without any force being applied to it by a bat or a hand.

In the same way, the devotion in the heart of the *jīvan mukta* goes on all the time naturally to the Lord and to the expression of the Lord as the total world of names and forms.

[Source: A.A. IX. 59]

202. THE MAN AND HIS HOUSE

Both Participation and Withdrawal are expressions of devotion alone in the *Jīvan Mukta.*

A man walks from one room to another in his house, moving things, arranging things, supervising activites etc.. The house serves as the "path" for his various activities.

Then he sits down to rest. Now the house is his abode. Thus the house is both his path and his abode, both the means and the end, depending on how he uses it.

In the same way, the *jīvan mukta*, whether he participates in the world or withdraws form it, it is as if he has already reached the abode of his being, the non-dual existence.

[Source: A.A. ix. 32]

203. THE TWO SLEEPING FRIENDS

The *Jñānī* (Knower) sees nothing other than the Self.

Two friends went to sleep side by side under a tree. One dreamt that both of them had gone on a long journey and had strange experiences.

On waking up, he told his friend all his dream experiences and asked: "Was it so?"

The friend only laughed at him, and said: "This was *your* dream. What *you* dreamt cannot affect *me*!"

In the same way, it is only the *ajñānī* (ignorant) who superimposes his own ignorance on the *jñānī* and mistakes him for a doer. In the state of *jñāna* (knowledge), the *jñānī* sees nothing separate from the Self.

The Self is ever shining and is only pure *jñāna* (knowledge).

[Source: TWRM. 499]

204. THE MAN WHO WALKED UP A JUNGLE PATH

Seeing the world with *Jñāna Dṛṣṭi* (Enlightened Vision).

A man wanted to visit a village on a hill. The path was steep and rough. But since he wore a pair of good strong shoes on his feet, he did not feel the pain of treading on stones and thorns.

In the same way, the *jñānī* who has acquired the *dūra dṛṣṭi* feels no more attachments even if he mixes with the world and moves about in it. Everything will be natural once this *jñāna dṛṣṭi* is attained.

What is there apart from the Self?
It is here.
All this is THAT.
We are in THAT only.
Being in IT, why search for IT?

Dṛṣṭam jñānamayim Kṛtvā paṣyet Brahmamayamjagat
When the vision is absorbed in *jñāna*, one sees the world as *Brahman.*

[Source: LSR. 83]

205. THE WOVEN CLOTH

The *Abheda Dṛṣṭi* of the *Jīvan Mukta.*

A lady had created a whole world of trees, flowers, animals, waterfalls, men, women and children on a cloth.

A child came by and, on pulling one end of the thread around the entire *"jagat"* which she had created out of her imagination, all that remained were yards and yards of mere thread. In that thread, the entire world had become one.

So also, the whole world is made of the material called Consciousness. He who has unwound the phenomenal world knows the Reality behind the world. To him, there are no more differences and distinctions.

There is no difference ever between *Brahman* and the *jagat* or between *Brahman* and the *jīva.* He who is established in this knowledge is a *jīvan mukta.*

He is liberated in life.

[Source: V.C. 440]

206. THE CHRYSANTHEMUM FLOWER

The *Jīvan Mukta's* vision of the world

The chrysanthemum is a fragrant flower with many petals. Its fragrance announces its presence. When the flower blooms, the thousand petals open slowly, whorl after whorl. Can we say that there are a thousand flowers and a thousand fragrances? The flower continues to be one.

In the same way, I, the Pure Consciousness, is manifesting as the experiencer-experience-experienced at millions of points, in a million ways, in a million sequences; but it remains one without a second.

The man of wisdom is firmly rooted in this vision.

[Source: A.A. IX 8]

207. THE LAMP IN A POT WITH HOLES

How a man of subtle perception sees the world.

It is a Deepavali night. Lights have been lit. One lighted candle has been kept inside a pot with holes.

One person looks at it and exclaims: "How beautiful it looks. So many points of light!" His companion seeing the same pot says: "It is just one source of light coming through the many holes."

The first person's vision is on the emerging points of light and the gaps of darkness between them, whereas the second person's attention is on the light; he does not see any gap between the holes.

In the same way, when a person with subtle and introverted intellect (the *divya puruṣa*) looks at the world, his perception is that of one-ness in spite of many-ness. This perception of many-ness creates no difference in his knowledge. When we see gaps between persons and beings, we are many; when we see that all of us are all one consciousness, "We *are all one.*" In this statement, "we" "are" and "all" are illusions; "one" is the Reality. In this knowledge, all differences of seer, seen and seeing are wiped out. This Pure Knowledge is "I am."

208. THE SUGARCANE THAT IS CUT

Every experience is a *prasāda* from the Lord.

A boy was given a sugarcane . He began to cut pieces from the long stick and eat it, beginning from the top. As he went on cutting further and further below, it tasted sweeter and sweeter.

In the same way, every experience in life, even if it is painful initially, is ultimately a step towards the Lord. The man of wisdom considers even the unhappy events in life as the Lord's *prasāda*, (His Grace).

[Source: A.A. IX. 19]

209. THE PORTER

Unloading the burden of relative existence.

A porter was carrying a heavy load on his head. He was weary. He came by a stone rest and unloaded his burden on to it. He sat down in relief, free from the exhaustion of carrying the load.

Similarly, the *dhīra puruṣa*, the man of wisdom, who understands that all the load of worldly relationships only take one away from the Lord, withdraws from (unloads) the burden of relative existence. He feels no more weighed down by *saṁsāra.* Neither participation in the world nor withdrawal from it is able to influence him any more. He has attained the State of Supreme Restfulness, where there is no fatigue, no tension, no worry. He is not involved in the world. He is totally absorbed in *Paramānanda* (supreme bliss).

[Source: P.D. XI-125-6]

210. THE ROCKS ON THE RIVER-BED

The man of wisdom abides firmly in Supreme Knowledge.

Huge rocks lie on the river-bed.

The river is constantly flowing around and above them, swirling and whirling and dashing against them. But the rocks stand firm, unmoving and un-movable.

In the same way, the names and forms keep constantly changing, but "I", (the *Brahman*), the support of all these modifications never change-s.

The man of wisdom therefore, stands rock-like in the Supreme Knowledge of the Self.

[Source: P.D. XIII-100]

211. THE HAND THAT OFFERED THE *'AHUTI'*

Discovery of the core of one's Being.

A person is offering oblation in the *yajña* (fire). Once the *āhuti* is dropped, the hand is withdrawn, for it has no more function.

In the same way, the words *sat, cit* and *ānanda* serve only a limited purpose of indicating the Truth. Once the Truth is revealed, they have no further utility; they disappear in the only place where sound can disappear - in the silence. This is the core of one's being, agitation-less bliss. *Amṛta Anubhava.*

[Source: A.A. 24-26]

Books and Cds available at :

Sharda Sangeet Vidyalaya
Nada Brahma Mandir
Madhoosudan Kelkar Marg
Bandra East,
Mumbai - 400 009
Ph. +22 - 26591838

Ajay Usha Kant
The Baby Shop
7/1 Ulsoor Road
Bangalore - 560 042
Ph. +80 - 5599503, 5586105

Yoga Vedanta Association Inc.
14, Meridian Parade
Wantirna South
Melbourne
Victoria-3152
61-03-9837 5995 Home.

Happy Folks Of South Africa
P.O. Box 131426,
Benoni, 1511
Republic of South Africa

Postal Address For Correspondence
Sat Bhavana Trust
128, Brij Kutir,
Dr. M.B.Raut Road, First Floor,
Shivaji Park, Mumbai - 400 028,
India.
Tel. No: +91-9820366088

Prabhu Mandhana
S-110 Lohadia Towers
Ashok Marg,
C Scheme
Jaipur - 302 001
Ph. +141 - 2376673

Be Happy Inc.
4169, Bludau Dr.,
Bldg 2410, Warrenton,
VA-20187, USA
(M) 001-703-470-9946

Mr. Prakash Modak
102, Parag, 1st Floor,
Near Andheri Sports Complex.
J.P. Road, Andheri (west),
Mumbai - 400 053
Tel. No. 022-26743330

Padam Chand Gupta
Rajlaxmi Commodities Pvt. Ltd
4033 1st Floor, Naya Bazar Delhi- 6
Mobile: 98100-75276
9873- 64300 (Santosh)
Mail: Padamchandgupta@gmail.com

OTHER BOOKS BY INDRA PUBLISHING HOUSE

Hindi Edition

कैरियर समाधान

अभिषेक खरे

विद्यार्थियों को सभी क्षेत्रों से सबंधित कैरियर के लिए उपयोगी दिशा निर्देश प्रदान करती यह पुस्तक।

मूल्य : 95/– मात्र

यह कैसी विदाई ...

डॉ. डी. यू. पाठक

यह कहानी है, कोख में पल रही दो भ्रूण कन्याओं की – 'दीदी' और 'छोटी' की। उनका वार्तालाप और छोटी के जिज्ञासा भरे प्रश्न आज की व्यवस्था पर करारे व्यंग्य हैं। ये आज भी अनुत्तरित हैं।

मूल्यः रू. 60/– मात्र

अंटार्कटिक आकर्षण क्यों?

डॉ. प्रमोद कुमार पुरोहित

अंटार्कटिक महाद्वीप के रहस्यों को उजागर करती यह पुस्तक। (रंगीन चित्रों सहित)

मूल्यः रू. 175/– मात्र

एक्यूप्रैशर फुट रिफ्लेक्सोलॉजी

डी.सी. वाझल्य

पाठक इस पुस्तक को पढ़कर स्वयं उपचार कर सकते है तथा उपचार केन्द्र भी खोल सकते है।

मूल्य : 195/– मात्र

इंडियन बिजनेस वुमन

शून्य से शिखर

प्रकाश बियाणी

इस पुस्तक में दी गई 22 सफल महिलाओं के जीवन की यशोगाथा आपको सोचने और कुछ महत्वपूर्ण करने के लिए प्रेरित करेगी।

मूल्य : (HB)325/– मात्र
(PB)195/– मात्र

मेनी लाइव्ज,मेनी मास्टर्स

डॉ. ब्रायन वीज़

एक मशहूर मनोवैज्ञानिक और उसकी युवा मरीज की पूर्वजन्म चिकित्सा की सच्ची कहानी, जिसने उन दोनों के जीवन को बदलकर रख दिया।

मूल्य : 150/– मात्र

English Edition

Before It's late

Dr. Vijay Agrawal

Students should read this book to know how to better manage their time.

Price: Rs. 95/- Only

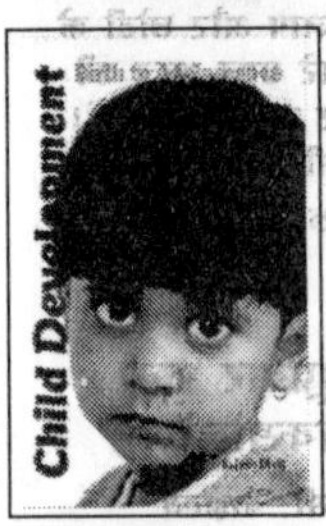

Child Development: Birth to Adolescence

Dr. Rajesh Dixit

This book is for new parents who wants to know about each & every development stage of their young ones.

Price : Rs. 150/- Only

Seven Spiritual Games of mind to succeed

Dr. M. L. Agarwal

Who am I ? You are you own architect. Play Seven Spiritual Games & win over yourself. It is self-discipline & self evolvement.

Price : 95/- Only

The Barefoot Indian

Julia Heywood

In this book eternal wisdom is expressed in the context of modern day to day life in a fresh, sensitive, intuitive, humorous and profoundly inspirational way.

Price: Rs. 80/- Only

Spoken English Made Easy w/cd

Deepali Gupta

This book will help you in developing writing skills, improving your vocabulary, grammar, expression & over all personality development.

Price: Rs. 150/- Only

Transcendental Vision of Sri Ram

Dr. M. L. Agarwal

The divine deeds of Sri Ram can be your guide to live a life in peace and bliss.

Price: Rs. 125/- Only

Antarctica : Where the silence speaks

Dr. Pramod Kumar Purohit

A book revealing all the mysteries of this continent.

Price: Rs. 195/- Only

Communication: A Path Way To Success

Ratna Juneja

This handy book is to make you master in communication. Must read for everyone.

Price: Rs. 60/- Only

Master Your Mind

Dr. Vijay Agrawal

A Practical book on "How To Control Your Mind".

Price: Rs. 250/- Only

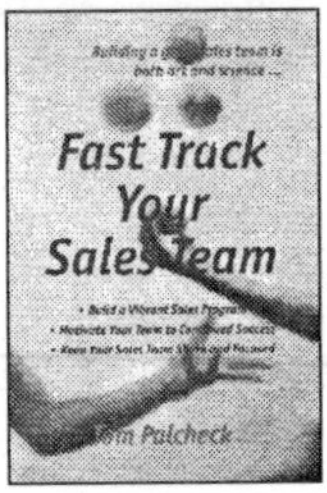

Fast Track Your Sales Team

Tom Palcheck

Throw out the old and replace it with a new, vibrant sales management style which will guarantee success for you and your team.

Price: Rs. 95/- Only

Who Loves Dies Well
Dharmavidya

In this book you will read the intimacy of Buddhist spiritual life, unique yet universal, laid bare by confrontation with death and a son's love for his mother in her final day

Price: Rs. 195/- Only

Can You Manage
Ivor Kenny

The point of the book is that, since few things are black and white, clear-cut, either/or, we have to manage in a way that accepts the existence of contradictory phenomena without trying to resolve them.

Price: Rs. 95/- Only

The Abundance Tree
Patricia Heyman

If you want to go beyond dreaming your dream to living your dream, then this book is for you.

Price: Rs. 75/- Only

Winning The Interview Game
Alan H. Nierenberg

If you treat the interviewing process like the "game" that it is and become good at it you'll win every time.

Price: Rs. 150/- Only

How To Be Happy
Jenny Smedley

Who knows what the human mind is capable of or where that mind may have dwelt before in time and space? Jenny writes with sincerity and conviction, and this book contains some compelling case histories.

Price: Rs. 125/- Only

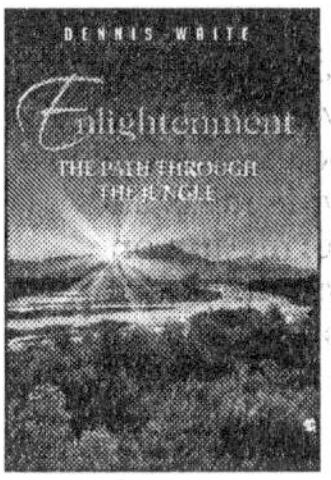

Enlightenment The Path Through The Jungle
Dennis Waite

What is enlightenment? What is it not? – exposes the myths and defines this misused term once and for all.

Price: Rs. 150/- Only

Who Rules In Your Life
Miriam Subirana

You can live every moment of your life knowing how to choose good and beneficial thoughts, and protect yourself from negative influences. You can do it by becoming aware of the way you think.

Price: Rs. 95/- Only

Patanjali's Art Of Meditation Yoga
Dr. M.L. Agarwal
Er. Sanjeev Agrawal

One who thinks of enlightenment is enlightened. One who thinks of bondage is bonded. There is a truthful popular folk wisdom "I am what I think of.

Price: Rs. 60/- Only

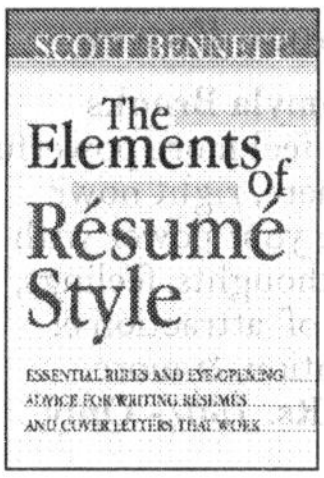

The Elements of Resume Style
Scott Bennett

The Elements of Résumé Style gives you more than 1,400 sample action words, action statements, and position descriptions, plus more than 700 words, phrases, and vague claims to avoid.

Price: Rs. 95/- Only

Dare To Live
Miriam Subriana

Learn how to become strong in your own right, how to stop comparing yourself to others. Learn to know yourself, and heal the wounds, let go the pain.

Price: Rs. 150/- Only

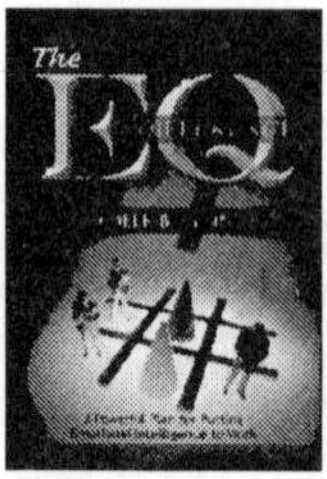

The EQ Difference

Adele B. Lynn

Emotional intelligence (EI) has been proven to be a leading driver of success.The EQ Difference shows you how to develop your own emotional quotient as well as that of your peers, employees, and even senior executives.

Price: Rs. 225/- Only

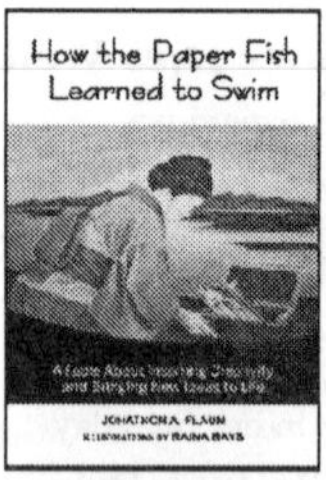

How The Paper Fish Learned To Swim

Johathon A. Flaum

This book presents a beautiful and unique fable as a springboard to unlocking creativity and innovation in the workplace.

Price: Rs. 125/- Only

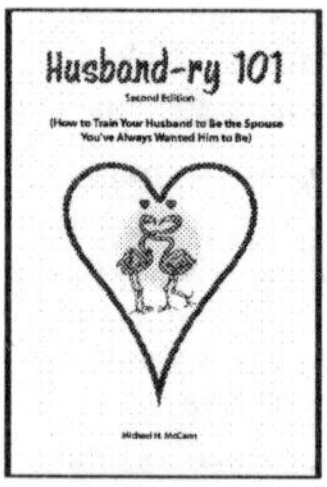

Husband-ry 101

Michael H. McCann

Husbandy 101 is a great gift for newlyweds and couples wanting to keep their marriage as fun as the day they became engaged.

Price: Rs.150/- Only

Travel Within

Jamshid Hosseini

A Spiritual guide for people from all walks of life.

Price: Rs.125/- Only

Talk Like A Winner

Steve Nakamoto

This book is designed to provide ideas and information on communication, relationships, and success.

Price: Rs.175/- Only

Men Are Like Fish

Steve Nakamoto

LOVE MADE FUN! Here is a simple way for women to understand men and land their elusive love.

Price: Rs.150/- Only

The POWER of Appreciation

Nelson & Calaba

"This is a powerful book for teaching you the simplicity and ease of using appreciation to create a better life than you can possibly imagine. You will be reading this over and over!

Price: Rs. 175/- Only

The Lost Art of General Management

Rob Waite

The Lost Art of General Management is a must read for anyone who wants to break out of the ranks of middle management.

Price: Rs. 95/- Only

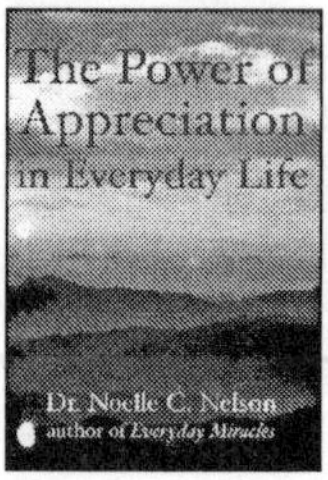

The Power of Appreciation In Everyday Life

Dr. Noelle C. Nelson

The Power of Appreciation explains the scientific foundation and principles of appreciation.

Price: Rs. 125/- Only

Choose Power

Pammyla Brooks

How can I feel more powerful right here, right now? Increase your power with people, thoughts, feelings, power of attraction & intention, & more.

Price: Rs. 150/- Only

The Mind Menu

Jonny Chuter

This is an empowering guide to help us create the life we want through the power of our thoughts.

Price: Rs. 195/- Only

Leadership Gurus speak out!

Adele Alfano and Kathy Glover Scott

This book presents you the collective wisdom, experience and knowledge of 13 experts, who are leader themselves.

Price: Rs. 195/- Only

The 7 Laws of Stress Management

Anthony D. Parnell

This is a workbook designed to learn seven steps to develop an effective stress management plan & increase productivity.

Price: Rs. 95/- Only

Power of Appreciation In Business

Noelle C. Nelson, Ph.D

Grow your business the same way Southwest Airlines, See's Candies and Ryder System, Inc. grow theirs: with the power of appreciation.

Price: Rs. 195/- Only

Emotional Intelligence

Jane Wharam

With this book, You can know yourself better, understand how to react in ways that improve the quality of your life.

Price: Rs. 125/- Only

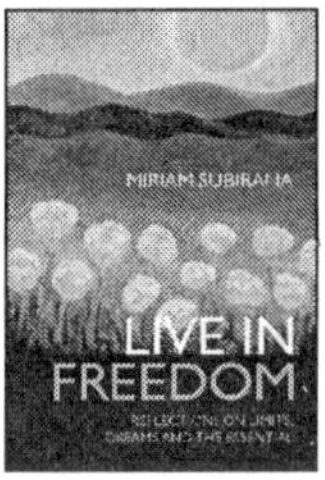

Live In Freedom

Miriam Subirana

More than a book, it is an invitation to go into oneself, to become aware of what we are, but above all, of what we can become.

Price: Rs. 125/- Only

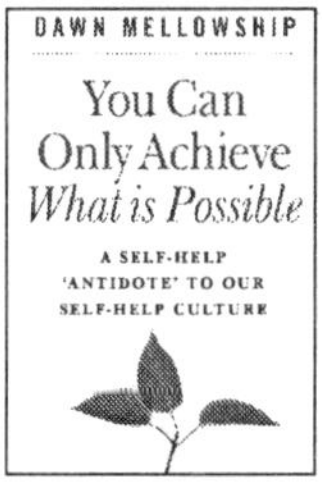

You Can Only Achieve What is Possible

Dawn Mellowship

Illustrated with practical exercises, this book contains stimulating advice to overcome the perceived obstacles blocking one's true purpose.

Price: Rs. 195/- Only

Achieving Unlimited Success

Dennis A. Kelley

This book will act as your guiding companion to help you achieve happiness and live a life of integrity.

Price: Rs. 195/- Only

The 'F' it way to Success and Happiness

Anne Hassett

Try a good old expletive like "F" word to achieve success & happiness in your life.

Price: Rs. 95/- Only

Palmistry

Johnny Fincham

This book draws on ground-breaking scientific research into individual fingerprint patterns & illustrated with images of actual hands.

Price: Rs. 150/- Only

Why Cats Don't Bark

Edie Raether

Why Cats Don't Bark gently nudges you in the direction of your own powerful intuitive abilities for optimal performance.

Price: Rs. 125/- Only

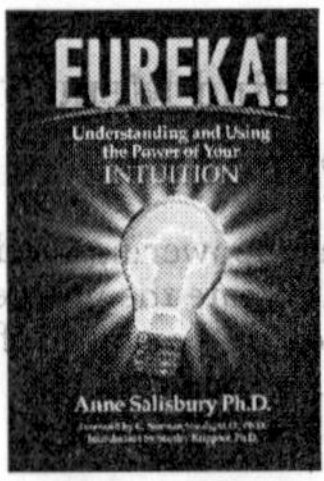

Eureka

Anne Salisbury

A book for all those who wish to enhance their intuition. Open any page get going with your own intuitive development.

Price: Rs. 225/- Only

How To Be A Great Sales Professional

Nido Qubein

Through this book discover the secrets of selling in today's tough sophisticated markets.

Price: Rs. 195/- Only

Never Be Late Again

Diana DeLonzor

It is a wonderfully practical book that combines instructive techniques with sound, simple exercises.

Price: Rs. 195/- Only

Peanut Butter and Jelly Management

Chris and Reina Komisarjevsky

"The Book is an absolute treasure trove ofmanagement information, insight, and guidance."

Price: Rs. 195/-Only

Play The Game of Life

Corinne Williams

Play the Game of Life just might be the lost user's guide to the biggest, most challenging game you ever came to play.

Price: Rs. 125/- Only

Viveka-Cudamani

Swami Anubhavananda

This great text on vedanta is attributed to Bhagawan Shankaracharya.

Price: Rs. 150/- Only

Forthcoming Book of Swami Anubhavananda

- **Choti Choti Batein**
- **Let Meditation Happen**